The *Complete Guide* to Buying a Property in Spain

by *Anthony I. Foster*

With very many thanks to Joan El Faghloumi (for compilation and interpretation) and to Susan Patterson (for layout and cover design), without whose help this book would never have come to fruition

I do hope that you will find this guide informative and concise, and that it will help you in buying the property of your dreams in Spain.

Should you find information contained herein which you feel needs updating, or if you have any comments or suggestions to make, please contact the author at the address below.

May I wish you very many happy years in your new home.

Anthony I. Foster
Nerja, Spain

7th Edition (revised) published June 2001
First published September 1994

©   **Property Search Spain**, Cambridge 1994
ISBN: 0 9523639 2 5

Property Search Spain, Sheraton House, Castle Park, Cambridge, CB3 0AX
Telephone: 01223 462244 Fax: 01223 460178
Also at: 'City Base' Telephone: 01223 370000 Fax: 01223 370040

CONTENTS

Chapter   *Page*

Preface

Introduction 1

1 Buying a Resale Property 5

2 Buying a New Property or a Plot of Land 17

3 Buying a Property in the Country or an Inherited Property 37

4 *Escritura* Costs 41

5 Community of Owners 49

6 Power of Attorney 53

7 Making a Spanish Will 55

8 *Residencia* and Work Permits 59

9 Spanish Driving Licences 69

10 Mortgages 73

11 Spanish Taxes 89

12 Selling Your Property in Spain 101

13 General Information 107

    Security

    Parking in Spain

    Traffic Department:

      Buying a Car or Motorbike, & Registration

    Vehicle Tax

    Building Permits

    Payment of Local Taxes

    Census Register

    Schools

    Water

    Electricity

    Telephone

    Doctors

    Banks

    Taking your Pets

    National Holidays

Glossary of Terms 137

List of Lawyers and Surveyors 143

So you are planning to buy a property in Spain or on one of her islands? *Don't do anything until you read this!*

Over the twenty years that I have lived in Spain, I have built up a network of tried and trusted estate agents virtually all around the coastal areas of the mainland of Spain and the islands.

As you have bought my book, let me now ensure that you deal with the right agents when you come over to buy a property in Spain. I will get in touch with my agent in the area that you are interested in and ask them to send you information. When you are coming over to look for property, I will arrange for them to meet you at the airport and, if required, ask them to organise accommodation for you.

You can get in touch with me directly in
Nerja, Malaga, Spain on:
Telephone/Fax: 00 34 952 523695   Mobile 00 34 629 577445

If you wish to speak to me personally, phone me between 4 and 7 p.m.
UK time, Monday to Friday, or fax me at any time.

I have contacts with agents in the following areas:
Costa del Sol, Costa Blanca, Costa Brava, Mallorca, Menorca and the
Canary Islands.

Please don't risk thousands of pounds of your
hard-earned savings!

Property Search Spain
Sheraton House, Castle Park, Cambridge CB3 OAX
Telephone: 01223 462244/370000
Fax: 01223 460178/370040

Preface

This book was written by Anthony I. Foster, who has lived in Spain since May 1981 running his own Estate Agency in Nerja, on the Costa del Sol. He is fluent in Spanish, and his experience of selling property in Spain, his knowledge of Spanish law, local authorities and the country's cultural behaviour generally, make him something of an expert on all aspects of property buying in Spain.

His reason for writing this guide was prompted by the number of people he had come into contact with over the years who had very sad tales to tell of their disastrous transactions, coupled with the obvious lack of knowledge that people had about buying property in Spanish territory. Very often he found that people, to save money, had not used a lawyer, and they had not thought about the existence, or possible whereabouts, of the property deeds (the 'Escritura'). He was amazed to find that in an 'alien' country, with very different laws and procedures, they had allowed themselves to be - incredibly, and inexplicably - so trusting! He met these 'victims' when it was, of course, already too late. He is attempting to ensure that anyone thinking of buying in Spain in the future could avoid any similar heartaches and very, very costly mistakes when taking the plunge into Spanish property buying.

Spanish law, and in particular tax laws, are constantly being revised, so the author cannot be held responsible for any changes that may occur in the future. He also advises that whoever is buying a property in Spain should always deal with a fully qualified and recommended lawyer to sort out the legalities. Towards the end of this book there is a list of lawyers & surveyors, most of which have been given to me by the Abbey National (Gibraltar) whose names appear on their panel, and they have kindly allowed me to include them in my book. As you will see, the lists cover all the coastal areas of Spain, plus the Canary and Balearic Islands.

By dealing with a lawyer, and with the help of this book, you will join the thousands of people who have already successfully bought a property in Spain, avoiding unscrupulous agents, developers or private vendors. This handy guide will put you firmly on the right path, telling you everything you could possibly need to know.

The lawyers, surveyors and mortgage companies listed in this book have not and do not pay any commission or fees to the author.

INTRODUCTION

So You're Buying a Property in Spain?

You have arrived at your destination in Spain, or perhaps one of her islands. You're looking forward to the sunshine, and it's All Systems Go! in the search for the home of your dreams. As you're relaxing and sipping your first beer or glass of wine, would you spare me a moment to heed some words of advice? Are you listening? Okay. What I would like to say to you is this: The first thing you must **not do** when you begin your search is to have, effectively, **booked your brains into the left luggage office at the airport**. You may laugh, yes, but it would seem so many people have done that very thing in the past.

There are always tragic stories in the national press and on television of people losing their life savings because they have dealt with an unscrupulous developer or estate agent. Or possibly they had met someone in a bar who had a property for sale, only to discover later that they didn't own it in the first place, or there were enormous debts on the property. I am so very aware of what can happen to people caught this way, and that is the reason for writing this book. Please try to ensure that you don't fall into the trap that has ensnared so many before in Spain. So, before I go into all the ins and outs of Spanish property purchase, here are just a few tips :

When you arrive at your destination, you will soon discover that just about everybody you meet is an expert, and apparently everyone does a bit of property selling. If you go into a bar or restaurant and happen to mention, in conversation, that you are in Spain to buy a property, Pepe the waiter will immediately tell you that he has a friend who has got a property for sale at a very good price, or he knows someone who will help you. Maybe you will be sitting in a bar and get into conversation with someone who lives there, and of course they will inevitably know someone who wants to sell, or they may even try to sell you their *own* property, if they have one. Obviously you must not get involved ... if anything goes wrong - and it probably will - you will have no comeback whatsoever.

You will find that there are many bar-room lawyers as well, and they *all* know everything there is to know about buying a property in Spain, *and* the tax system. Take no notice of these characters, because at the most you will get only half-truths and an awful lot of incorrect information.

So what *should* you do? Well, first off, unless you are on an inspection flight with a reputable agency from England and being met by their agents in Spain, you should spend a little bit of time looking around the town or village where you are planning to buy, and find the area you like most and where you think you would like to have a property; then look for 'For Sale' signs, and contact the agency handling the property sale.

Don't be afraid to ring the number you see on the sign, as they will almost certainly speak English. Once you have made contact with the estate agents, you will obviously soon get a feel if he/she is basically honest, but it's a good idea to ask if they are registered with the local College of Estate Agency Lawyers. In Spanish, this would be *Agente de propiedad Inmobiliaria*, and they should be able to show you a certificate of their registration and their A.P.I. Number. This is most important, as it means that they have a registered Estate Agency lawyer working with them and they are not only registered with the College, but have had to place a bond with the College, which means that if anything goes wrong, they can be sued.

This will certainly give you a lot more confidence when you find the property you wish to buy.

If you don't see any 'For Sale' signs on properties in the area you like, it does not mean that there are no properties for sale in that area - it is probably because the owners do not want the estate agent to put up a board. Therefore, do not hesitate to call into estate agents' offices and enquire if they have any properties available in your chosen area. If you do call into an estate agents office - and I can't repeat this often enough - please ensure that they are a properly registered A.P.I. Agent. Details of their registration and relevant number should be on the sign outside the office, on the exterior of the building, or in the window display. Look for a 3 or 4 figure number.

Do not be misled by seeing names such as *Costa del Sol Properties* - it does not mean that they are registered estate agents. They must show you some proof that they are registered. Even if you are dealing with a fully registered estate agent, this does not mean that you are 100% safe - you should still employ a lawyer. Unfortunately in Spain there are lawyers and lawyers, so make sure that you use a lawyer that has been recommended to you by somebody who has previously bought a property successfully through a lawyer. Even then it's a good idea to refer to my book, to ensure that he is doing his job properly, and checking all the documentation that is mentioned in the book.

Okay, let us assume that you have been looking at properties with the agent and you have finally found the property you want to buy. What is the procedure now? Before we proceed, let me explain that the Spanish system is different to the English system of buying a property - in Spain, you are not dealing with solicitors who draw up and exchange contracts on completion. In Spain, all Deeds for properties are drawn up by Public Notaries. Unlike in England,

Public Notaries are very important people and are responsible for legalising many documents, including Deeds ('*Escritura*' in Spain), Powers of Attorney, etc. They are appointed by the Government and are qualified lawyers who have gone on to study to become Notaries. Also, unlike in England, on finding the property you wish to buy, a Sale & Purchase Contract is drawn up and a deposit is paid, which fixes the price, so you cannot be gazumped. This is completely binding on both parties.

The Contract includes the date of the final payment and the signing of the Public *Escritura*. The *Escritura* is signed in the Notary's Office and witnessed by the Notary and legalised with his signature. All parties who are involved must be present to sign the *Escritura*; that is to say, if the property being purchased is in the names of, for example, the husband and wife - in the case of the vendor - and you and your wife are purchasing in joint names, all four people must be present, or have a Power of Attorney, in Spanish, authorising the husband, for example, to sign for his wife if she is unable to attend.

You've probably spent half a lifetime reaching this monumental decision; you're very excited at the prospect of owning your very own place in the sun, so please don't spoil it for yourself. Give it plenty of thought before you proceed - and tread carefully! If you follow the guidelines laid down in this book, I promise you that you will not go wrong in your transaction.

Happy Hunting!

CHAPTER 1

Buying a Resale Property

Buying a second-hand, or 'resale' property, is the most common category of property purchase and so, logically, I have begun with this.

The normal procedure when you have found the property you wish to buy is that a Contract of Sale & Purchase is drawn up and a deposit is paid, normally 10% of the agreed sale price, and the contract is signed by both the Vendor/Vendors, and Purchaser/Purchasers. On the signing of the contract and the payment of the deposit, this commits both parties to the price and conditions of the Contract.

The Contract would be drawn up either by the estate agent or your lawyer. If it is drawn up by the estate agent, it is always advisable to let your lawyer vet the contract before signing, and before parting with your deposit money. Before signing the Contract, ensure that you know the amount of the community fees, as on some *urbanizaciones* these fees can be quite high - anything up to £1,500 per year. Also ask for a break-down of the approximate costs of the *Escritura* and any other incidental charges. It is better to know costs before you buy - you don't want to get a nasty surprise after the event. Also, you should ask to see the following:

•   A copy of the *Escritura* (Deeds). This shows you that the people who claim to be the owners are the people named on the *Escritura*.

- A *Nota Simple*. This is a document from the Land Registry office showing who the legally registered owner/s of the property are and if there are any mortgages or other encumbrances registered against the same. The name/s on the *Nota Simple* should of course match the name/s on the *Escritura*. If this is not the case, it could mean that they do not own the property, maybe having already sold it to someone else, or their *Escritura* could not be registered for some reason. Before going any further you must consult a lawyer.

Once you have seen these documents and are satisfied that the property belongs to the people who claim to be the owners, and that there are no mortgages or other encumbrances, you can now proceed to the Contract. *However*, before signing, and paying the deposit, you should ensure that the following is included in the Contract :

1.   The price and conditions of payment, clearly written.

2.   All charges on the property, i.e. community fees; electricity bills; telephone bills; water bills (which may be included in the community fees); and annual rates, all of which are ***the responsibility of the vendor up until the day of the signing of the public Escritura***.   This is most important, as all debts in Spain are on the property, and **not** the person; You, the purchaser, are only responsible for any debts on the property from the day of the signing of the *Escritura* and the handing over of the keys. Therefore, it is of the utmost importance that you see proof that any outstanding debts, such as community fees, or annual rates, are up to date before signing the *Escritura* and handing over the final payment.

3.   A complete description of the property, i.e. lounge/diner, kitchen, guests' toilet, 3 bedrooms, bathroom, terraces etc. The total square meterage of both the plot and the apartment, house or villa. The reason for this is that maybe the present owners have extended the property, perhaps adding a bedroom, or converted a basement into a self-contained apartment. Therefore the description of the property in the Contract should match the description of the property in the *Escritura*. If it does not, the present owners must have a building licence for this work and it will be their responsibility to pay the costs of the declaration of new building at the Notary's Office, including the Land Registry fees, when the *Escritura* is made in your name. In the case that there is no planning permission for the extension, then you must get your lawyer to check with the Town Hall to ascertain if this work can be legalised. In the case that it can, of course the present owners will be responsible for all costs.

4.   The full registration details of the Land Registry, the *Finca* No. (The Land Registration No.), the book No. and all the other registration details. This information is obtainable from either the *Escritura* or the *Nota Simple*.

5.   There should be a section in the contract headed *Cargas* (charges). This of course should read as Free of Charges and Encumbrances, and if in the case that there is a mortgage on the property, this should be reflected here. If you do not wish to take over the mortgage but would like it paid off, this should be taken up in the Conditions of Payment section of the contract, which should be reflected as follows:

The amount owing on the existing mortgage, including all the cancellation costs, will be deducted from the final payment. In this way you can ensure that the mortgage is paid in full and the costs of the cancellation are covered. Your lawyer or estate agent will obtain the amount owing to the Bank on the date agreed for completion and the cancellation costs for the Notary and Land Registry fees. They will also arrange for the representative of the Bank to attend the Notary's Office to sign the deed of cancellation of the mortgage, and this is normally done on the same day and just prior to you signing your *Escritura*. The document cancelling the mortgage must be signed by the Notary prior to you signing your *Escritura*.

6.   There should be a clause in the Contract headed *Arrendamiento* (sitting tenants). This of course should read that it is free of sitting tenants.

7.   If the property is being sold furnished, which is normally the case when buying a resale property in Spain, a complete inventory should be drawn up and signed by both parties and this document should be annexed to the contract. This will ensure that there are no nasty surprises when you return to sign the *Escritura* and, on checking the property, find there is no furniture... If the vendors are Spanish, it is quite possible that the property will be sold unfurnished. If this is the case, ask for a list of exactly what they are taking. I have come across cases where the property was being sold unfurnished and the vendors have not only taken the furniture, curtains and light fittings, they have removed all the kitchen units, cooker, fridge and washing machine as well. It is a good idea to visit the property just prior to completion to ensure that what has previously been agreed will be left in the property is actually there.

8. Under recent new Spanish legislation, the purchaser is obliged to retain 5% of the value declared on the *Escritura*. It is very important that this is also taken up in the Contract of Sale & Purchase. The 5% retention *only* applies if the vendor is non resident in Spain; in other words, if the vendor *does not* have residential status in Spain at the time of selling, or has owned the property for the period of time (as explained on page 12).

9. The Contract will normally contain a penalty clause which states that if the balance outstanding is not paid by the agreed date specified in the contract, the purchaser will lose the amount paid and the vendor is free to offer the property for sale. The purchaser has no call against the property. So before you sign the Contract and pay the deposit, you must be sure that you can pay the balance on the agreed date.

10. Although it is unlikely that the vendor will back out of the sale at the last minute after signing the Contract, this is always a possibility, so it is not such a bad idea to have a further penalty clause inserted in the Contract, that if for any reason the vendors do not complete on the Contract and wish to withdraw, they must pay to the purchasers an indemnity of double the amount paid as a deposit for the purchase of the property in question. In fact, under Spanish law they must return double the amount already paid, or they can be forced by the Courts to complete the sale of the property to you.

11. If the property you are buying was built within the last 5-6 years, it is a good idea to ask to see proof that a building licence was obtained and that a certificate of the termination

of the building (*Certificado de fin de obra*) and the licence of first occupation (*Licencia de primera ocupacion*) have been issued. These documents or proof of the same can be obtained from the local Town Hall. You could run into difficulties if these documents have not been obtained and paid for.

The vendor is now obliged to present the last receipt of payment of the *contribuciones* or I.B.I. (annual rates) at the Notary's, prior to the signing of the *Escritura*, and it is photocopied onto official Notarial paper and included in the *Escritura*. However, it is possible that there are previous years rates still outstanding, so it is a good idea to obtain a certificate from the local Rates Office (*Recaudacion Provincial*) stating that there are no outstanding rates to be paid.

With regard to the annual Community Fees, it is now necessary to obtain a certificate from the Administrator of the Community showing that the Community Fees are paid up to date on the property that you are purchasing. This is for the Notary, and your lawyer or estate agent should obtain this certificate for you and present it to the Notary, along with all the other documentation necessary for him to prepare the *Escritura*.

It has always been a normal practice of mine to obtain a *Nota Simple* from the Land Registry office on the day of the signing of the *Escritura*. This is to ensure that no debts or mortgages have been registered on the property since the initial search was made, when the contracts were drawn up and a deposit was paid. This is not necessary now, as the Notary's Office are obliged to obtain, by fax, a document from the Land Registry Office showing if there are any debts registered against the property, or if it is free of encumbrances.

You will of course need to open a Spanish Bank account, for paying standing orders such as electricity bills, community fees and so on. This is not difficult to do, all you need is to choose a bank, present your passport and give them your address in the U.K. You will need to pay in a small sum to activate the account. Most of the Banks have English speaking staff, particularly around the coastal areas of Spain.

If the property that you are buying is foreign-owned, the vendors will almost certainly want payment in their country's currency, for example in Sterling, German Marcs or whatever the currency may be. This of course is quite normal practice and perfectly legal. In fact, if two foreign people are involved in the Sale & Purchase of a property, it only complicates the issue when you get to the Notary's Office if the payment is being made in pesetas.

In my experience, the easiest and safest way to make the final payment is by way of a Bankers Draft, made payable to the vendor(s) and to bring this with you when you travel to Spain to sign the *Escritura*. You might be asking "What is a Bankers Draft?" A Bankers Draft is not a personal cheque - it is a Bank cheque, and payment is guaranteed in any Bank in the world, so there is no reason why the Vendor should refuse payment in this way.

If the property that you are buying is being sold in Pesetas/Euros, then of course you would get your Spanish bank to issue the bankers draft for the final payment. If this is the case, please make sure that you allow enough time for the funds to be transferred to your Spanish account for the completion. When transferring funds to Spain ask your bank in the U.K. to make a Swift telex transfer, rather than a normal telex transfer, as this will ensure that the funds are available in your Spanish bank account within four working days. Before handing over the Bankers Draft to the Vendor, you must insist on seeing all receipts for electricity, community fees, annual rates, water, and if it applies, telephone; and proof that the *Plus Valia* was paid by the Vendors, when they originally purchased the property. Under recent new legislation, a *Nota Simple* (a simple copy of the details of the property registered at the Land Registry Office) must now be obtained by the Notary's Office, to be received on the day of the signing of the *Escritura*. This must be organised with the Notary's Office at least three days before the signing.

The Bankers Draft should be handed over *after* the signing of the *Escritura*, and I would suggest is dealt with in the following manner:

If you are not using the services of a lawyer, but you are buying through an estate agent whom you *trust* (I must assume you do, otherwise you wouldn't be buying from him in the first place!) - give him the Bankers Draft just prior to going to the Notary's Office and he can then hand it over to the Vendor after the signing of the *Escritura*. In this way the Vendor does not receive payment until such time as the *Escritura* is signed and he has the guarantee of receiving payment from the estate agent after the signing, and knows not only that the Bankers Draft is made out in his name, but also that a Bankers Draft is the same as receiving cash.

You are probably asking yourself "Why don't I just hand the Bankers Draft over at the signing of the *Escritura*?" Well, very simply, because the property is being sold in foreign currency, it technically has to be paid outside the country; so as to overcome any problems, at the time of the signing of the *Escritura*, we tell the Notary that the payment was made before this act - for example, in London, if one or both of the parties is English - although the reality is that it is being paid in Spain. The Notary is no doubt very aware that the payment is actually being made in Spain, but as he does not see it and as it is not illegal, he turns a blind eye.

Do not forget that the 5% retention has to be deducted from the amount owing. That is to say, 5% of the agreed amount that is being declared on the *Escritura* must be deducted from the balance. With reference to the 5% retention, this does not apply if the Vendor has *Residencia* in Spain and can prove to the Notary that he/she not only has a valid *Residencia* card, but can prove that they are paying their annual taxes in Spain. They must produce a certificate from the Spanish tax authorities to prove this. If they cannot produce this certificate or some other proof, you must retain 5% of the declared value. If you are buying from somebody who claims to have *Residencia*, do get your lawyer to check that they not only hold a current Resident's card, but they can prove that they are paying their annual taxes in Spain. If the property in question has been owned by an individual or individuals and was purchased on or before 31 December 1986, there is NO retention. If the property in question has been owned by a company and was purchased before 31 December 1976, there is NO retention. There is also no retention if the vendor is Spanish. If the property was purchased after these dates by the Vendor, the 5% retention still applies, at least until such time as the Spanish Tax authorities decide to make any further alteration to the law.

The 5% retention will be taken up in the Tax section of this book. It is not a bad idea to arrange the transfer of the 5% retention to your Bank in Spain well before you arrive in Spain for the signing, to ensure that the transfer has been received in good time to sign the *Escritura*.

Let us assume that you have now signed the *Escritura* and have handed over the Bankers Draft and are now the happy legal owners of your property in Spain. Well done!

But there's a *little* bit more to come.

What's the next step? You now have to pay the costs of the *Escritura*, and obtain a *Copia Simple* - yes, as it sounds: a simple copy of your *Escritura*. In some cases it may be that the Notary's Office will be able to prepare your *Copia Simple* immediately and let you know the costs, or you may have to return in a few days to collect it and pay the costs involved. After making the payments, the Notary's Office will send the original copy of your *Escritura* to the Land Registry Office for them to register the fact that you are the new owners of the property. After a period of some 2-3 months, your *Escritura* will be returned to the Notary's Office, duly registered. The time it takes to register your *Escritura* can vary, according to the amount of work that the Land Registry Office has at that time.

All the *Escritura* costs, the Notary's fees, Land Registry fees and the 6% transfer tax must be paid within 28 working days of the signing of the *Escritura*. If they are not paid within this period, fines will be levied for late payment. This also applies to the 5% retention. A longer period is normally given for the payment of the *Plus Valia*. However, my advice is to pay all these costs as soon as you know the amounts that you have to pay.

Once the *Escritura* has been returned to the Notary's Office, you can go along and pick up the original. All you have to produce is your *Copia Simple* and proof of identity; you can then take away your registered *Escritura*.... Congratulations! In addition, you might get a nice surprise and receive a small refund from the registration of your *Escritura*, as the amount paid for the registration is a deposit and they normally ask for more than is needed to cover this fee.

Once you have obtained your *Copia Simple* of the *Escritura*, you will need to take a few photocopies. These are :

* for payment of the *Plus Valia* Tax at the local Town Hall

* to change the *Contribuciones* (annual rates) to your name

* to transfer the electricity contract to your name

* to transfer the water contract to your name

* to transfer or obtain a telephone.

The relevant forms will have to be filled in and signed. This may not be easy for you but, as stated in the **Escritura Costs** chapter later on in this book, the agent you are buying the property through should make the necessary photocopies for you, and either go along with you to the various offices, or do so on your behalf.

If by any chance you should lose what is classed as the original of your *Escritura*, it is not too much of a disaster, as the Notary's Office actually retains the original that you all signed and what is called a First Copy of the *Escritura* is sent to the Land Registry Office. So you can always obtain another copy from the Notary's Office where you originally signed.

The costs involved in obtaining the *Escritura* will be explained in Chapter 4, entitled **Escritura Costs**.

* * *

CHAPTER 2

Buying a New Property or a Plot of Land

This chapter will deal with the purchase of a new property, with new property falling into four distinct categories :

I   A property to be constructed from plans from a developer
II   A property already under construction
III   A property that has recently been completed, but never lived in
IV   Buying a plot of land and building your own property

I   *A Property to be Constructed from Plans from a Developer*

Buying a property that is going to be built for you is quite complicated, as the documentation required is extensive and even more care must be taken than when buying a resale property, or one that has been completed. However, the advantages of having a villa, for example, built to your own specification and where you are choosing the tiles for the kitchen - not to mention the possible positioning of certain rooms - probably outweigh the disadvantages. Because buying a new property can be complicated, you would certainly be well advised to use the services of a lawyer, and preferably one that has been recommended to you.

Before handing over a deposit and signing a contract, you must ask to see a *Nota Simple* from the Land Registry Office, showing proof that the person from whom you are buying the property is the registered owner of the land, and that there are no mortgages or encumbrances on the land. You must also see proof that a building licence has been obtained from the local Town Hall, and paid for. Furthermore, it makes sense to have some idea of the costs of the *Escritura*, including the *Plus Valia* Tax, before signing the contracts. This ensures you don't get any nasty shocks when you come to paying for it. This, in fact, applies to all categories of buying a property covered in this chapter.

Another important thing to remember is that when you are buying a property from a Developer/Builder, they will almost certainly try to persuade you to declare a much lower figure than you are paying to be shown on the *Escritura*. It is common practice in Spain to under-declare the value of the property that you are buying, but you should not declare less than 75-80% of the price you are paying and, if possible, the actual amount you are paying for the property. Always check through your lawyer, or the Notary's Office, what the minimum figure is that should be declared. Remember, when you come to sell the property, you will be paying 35% Capital Gains Tax on the difference you declared when you bought the property, and the declared value when you sell. The amount that you wish to declare on the *Escritura* should be made clear to the Developer/Builder at the contract stage.

It is imperative that all payments are made to the Developer/Builder by your Spanish Bank, because you will need a certificate for the Notary's Office showing that the funds to purchase the property have been imported in foreign currency.

Let us assume that you have chosen the plot of land. Plans have been drawn up and are to your satisfaction. Now we come to the Contract. It is very important that all the following details are taken up in this Contract:

i.   The total square meterage of the land/plot, the square meterage of the house/villa, and the total price, when the building is completed and ready for you to move into;

ii.   The deposit, which is normally 25% of the total price, and the stage payments - which are normally 25% on the completion of the roof; 25% on the tiling of the bathroom and kitchen; 25% on the completion of the building, the signing of the *Escritura* and the handing over of the keys;

iii.   Stage payments will only be released to the Developer/ Builder on receipt of an Architects' Certificate, stating that this particular stage of the building has been completed. If you are not in Spain while the building is going on, and will not be in Spain to make the stage payments, then you must leave instructions with your Spanish bank to release the stage payments to the Developer/Builder *only* on receipt of these certificates - I really must stress how important this is.

iv.   The Developer/Builder is responsible for the following payments :

- Building Licence (*Licencia de Obra*) which is obtained from the Planning Department of the local Town Hall;

- Architects & Surveyors fees for a complete project for the building of the house/villa and when the building is completed;

- The Certificate for the termination of the building; and the Licence of first occupation of the house/villa (*Certificado de Fin de Obra* and the *Licencia de Primera Ocupacion*, respectively).

- *The Boletin de Instalacion* (Certificate of installation) issued by the *Delegacion de Industria* (Delegation of Industry) for the electricity and water installations. You will need copies of these certificates to obtain the electric and water meters.

v.   All the registration details of the land where your property is being built must be included. For example, the *Finca* No. (The Land No. in the Land Registry), the Book No. etc. This information can be obtained from either the *Escritura* of the land/plot or the *Nota Simple* (The Registration Document from the Land Registry).

vi.   The Developer/Builder has an insurance policy to cover the possibility of him going bankrupt before he completes the building of your property, or he goes bankrupt before all the facilities on the complex are completed, i.e. roads, swimming pool and suchlike. The details of the insurance policy and the number of the policy and what it covers should also be included in the Contract. This is of paramount importance, as otherwise you could finish up with a half-built house, or your house completed but the complex only half finished.

vii.   A detailed plan of the property, with all the dimensions, and a specification of the building, with prices where applicable of floor and wall tiles per square metre. In fact, a very detailed specification of the building and installations is required, specifically to ensure there are no hidden extras appearing during the construction of the property. The plans and specification should be annexed to the Contracts and signed by all parties. In Spanish, this is called a *Memoria de Calidades*.

viii.   If a kitchen is being installed, then a detailed plan must be pre-
        pared, showing exactly what is being fitted and what domestic
        appliances are included. Also, it should be made clear that taps
        and connections of the plumbing are included. This should
        also be annexed to the Contract and signed by all parties.

ix.   If you are having a gas cooker or the water heating is by gas,
        the gas installation should be included. Also the inspection
        and contract for the gas, payment of which is the responsi-
        bility of the Developer/Builder, should also be reflected
        either in the Contract or specification.

x.   Electric, water and sewage is installed and that there are no
        connection charges. You should only pay for the installation
        of electric and water meters and for the actual gas cylinders,
        if Town Gas is not available.

xi.   If, as is normal in Spain, the garden is being landscaped, this
        should also be specified in the Contract or the building spec-
        ification.

xii.   It should also be clearly specified in the Contract what is
        your quota of participation in the Community of Owners. If
        the Community has not yet been formed, at least you will
        know what percentage you will have to pay towards the fees,
        and if the Community has already been formed, ask what
        your fees will be, as these can often be high - as much as
        £1,000 - £1,500 per year, depending on the services and
        facilities included in the Community charges.

xiii.   The Developer/Builder is responsible for the payment of all
        debts on the land, i.e. *Contribuciones* (Annual Rates) up until
        the time that you take possession of the property.

xiv.   A penalty clause will no doubt be included in the Contract that, if you fail to meet the payments agreed therein, the contract becomes null and void and you not only lose the amounts already paid but the Developer/Builder will be free to offer your property for sale to another party. So, as stated in the chapter dealing with the purchase of a resale property, you must be sure that you will be able to meet these payments.

xv.   A further penalty clause should be included in the Contract, which states that if the building is not completed on the date agreed in the Contract, then the Developer/Builder must pay an indemnity for each day after the completion date. The sum per day must be negotiated with the Developer/Builder and reflected in the Contract. It should be enough to cover, for example, the cost of a daily rate for you and your family to stay in a hotel until such time as the building is completed. (As you can see, if you proceed in the correct way with a property purchase, you are very well protected should anything go slightly awry!)

xvi.   It should be made clear in the Contract that you are only responsible for the payment of the costs of the *Escritura* for the sale and purchase of the property, not the segregation (*Segregacion*) and the declaration of the new building. The developer should pay the costs of the *Segregacion* (separating your land from the rest of the *Urbanizacion*), *Declaracion de Obra Nueva* (Declaring the new building) and you should only pay the costs of the *Compra/Venta* (Sale & Purchase) at the Notary's Office when the *Escritura* is drawn up.

xvii.   You should ask to see proof that the *Contribuciones* are paid up to date before handing over the final payment and signing the *Escritura*.

If you request any alterations or additions to the property that is under construction, you must always ask for a written quotation, and this should be signed by both parties, to save any disputes on 'extras' when the building is completed. Any major alterations or additions may also extend the completion date of the building. If this is the case, a new completion date should be agreed in writing and signed by both parties, as this will obviously affect the penalty clause for late completion in the Contract.

****

Note:

All the documents I have mentioned are of the utmost importance, because without the Certificate of the termination of the building, you will not be able to make the *Escritura* for the declaration of the new building at the Notary's Office, and without the licence of first occupation, you will not be able to get an electricity meter installed for your property - and therefore no electricity supply.

The certificate of the termination of the building is issued by the architect, a copy of which is presented to the Planning Department of the local Town Hall. This document informs the Planning authorities that the building has been finished in accordance with the plans presented when the original planning application was made. The Planning Department then sends an Inspector to have a good look at the building to see if it agrees with these plans and they then issue the Licence of first occupation. You should of course also receive copies of these documents. It should be clearly stated in the Contract that the Developer/Builder is not only responsible for obtaining these documents, but is also responsible for their payment.

When you are buying a new property which is being built for you by the Developer/Builder, or any new property, it is very important when the building is completed that the Developer/ Builder registers your property with the *RECAUDACION PROVINCIAL* (The Local Rates Office). This is also something that could be included in the Contract, where he commits himself to do this on the completion of the building. In fact, now many Town Halls in Spain and her islands will NOT issue the *Licencia de Primera Ocupacion* (The Licence of First Occupation) without seeing proof that the property that has been built has been registered with the *RECAUDACION PROVINCIAL* (The Rates Office) and of course without the *Licencia de Primera Ocupacion*, you will neither be able to sign the *Escritura* (Deeds) nor obtain your electric meter.

****

II   *A Property already under Construction*

A property that is under construction, but unfinished, is less complicated than actually having the property built from plans, but there are of course still pitfalls. So, I will explain what is involved with regard to buying a property in this category. Before a contract is drawn up and signed, you must obviously see proof that the Developer/Builder is the legal owner of the land, so you should ask to see a copy of the *Escritura* and a *Nota Simple* - not only proving ownership, but also to see that there are no mortgages or other encumbrances on the land.

Let us assume that the house you are interested in buying is constructed to the roof level. What should be in the Contract?

i.   As with purchasing a plot of land and having the property built, there must be a Building Licence (*Licencia de Obra*) and you must have details of the Building Licence in the Contract, which is that at the completion of the building, the Developer/Builder is responsible for the payment and obtaining this document, as with the Certificate of the termination of the building (*Certificado de Fin de Obra*), the Licence of First Occupation (*Licencia de Primera Ocupacion*) and the Certificate of Installation (*Boletin de Instalacion*) issued by the Delegation of Industry (*Delegacion de Industria*) for the electricity and water installations. You will need copies of these Boletins to obtain your electric and water meters.

ii.   The total square meterage of the land/plot and the total constructed area of the property, plus terraces.

iii   The full registration details of the land/plot, for example the *Finca* number (the registration no. of the land/plot), the book number etc. This information can be obtained from the *Escritura* (Deeds) for the land/plot or the *Nota Simple* (the copy of the Land Registry document).

iv. Of course, the price for the property should be clearly stated and the payment structure shown in detail. Under normal circumstances, it is quite possible that as the house is technically already half-built, the Developer/Builder will ask for 50% as a deposit, with the balance being paid on the completion of the building, handing over of the keys and the corresponding *Escritura*.

v. Again, as in the case of having a house constructed, it is of vital importance that the Developer/Builder has an insurance policy to cover the possibility of going bankrupt, for example, and not being able to complete either the house or the *Urbanizacion*. So details of this Insurance must be stated in the Contract.

vi. A detailed plan, with dimensions of rooms etc. and a full specification of the installations, i.e. tiles, with the price per square metre, must be annexed to the Contract and signed by all parties. In Spanish this is called a *memoria de calidades*.

vii. If the kitchen is being fitted, then a full specification should also be annexed to the Contract with plans, and if taps, plumbing connections and the installation for gas and the corresponding contract for the gas cylinders is included in the price.

viii. Electricity, water and sewerage is connected to the property and there are no connection charges. You should only pay for the installation of the electric meter, water meter and gas cylinders.

ix. If the garden is being landscaped, this should also be reflected in the Contract or specification.

x. Your quota of participation in the Community of Owners should be clearly specified in the Contract.

xi. As with all contracts, there will no doubt be a penalty clause that if you do not meet the payments as specified in the Contract, the Contract becomes null and void, and you lose whatever you have already paid, leaving the Developer/Builder free to offer the property for sale again. So you must be sure, before you sign the Contract, that you will be able to make the payments as agreed.

xii. A penalty clause should be included, which states that if the building is not completed on the agreed date, that the Developer/Builder should pay you as an indemnity a fixed sum for each day after the completion date. It should be enough to cover your expenses to stay in a hotel until the building is completed.

xiii. When the *Escritura* is drawn up, you should only be responsible for the costs for the Sale & Purchase (*Compra/Venta*) and not the Declaration of the new building, or the segregation of the land (*Segregacion de la Finca*). This should also be clearly stated in the Contract.

xiv.   The Developer/Builder is responsible for all debts on the property until the handing over of the keys and the *Escritura*.

xv.   As I have said before, It is a good idea to ascertain what the approximate costs of the *Escritura* will be and the *Plus Valia* Tax before signing the contract, to ensure you don't get a nasty surprise when you go to pay for it. It is imperative that all payments are made to the Developer/Builder through your Spanish Bank, as you will need a certificate from the Bank for the Notary's Office, showing that the funds have been imported into Spain.

It is imperitive that all payments are made to the developer/builder through your Spanish bank, as you will require a certificate from your bank for the Notary, showing that the funds for the purchase of the property have been imported into Spain.

If you request any alterations or additions to the property that is under construction, you must always ask for a written quotation, and this should be signed by both parties, to save any disputes on 'extras' when the building is completed. Any major alterations or additions may also extend the completion date of the building. If this is the case, a new completion date should be agreed in writing and signed by both parties, as this will obviously affect the penalty clause for late completion in the Contract.

****

Note:

All the documents I have mentioned are of the utmost importance, because without the Certificate of the termination of the building, you will not be able to make the

Escritura for the declaration of the new building at the Notary's Office, and without the licence of first occupation, you will not be able to get an electricity meter installed for your property - and therefore no electricity supply.

The certificate of the termination of the building is issued by the architect, a copy of which is presented to the Planning Department of the local Town Hall. This document informs the planning authorities that the building has been finished in accordance with the plans presented when the original planning application was made. The Planning Department then sends an Inspector to have a good look at the building to see if it agrees with these plans and they then issue the Licence of first occupation. You should of course also receive copies of these documents. It should be clearly stated in the Contract that the Developer/Builder is not only responsible for obtaining these documents, but is also responsible for their payment.

When you are buying a new property, which is under construction, it is very important that the Developer/Builder registers the new building with the *RECAUDACION PROVINCIAL* (The Rates Office). This should be reflected in the contract as his responsibility, as many Town Halls in Spain and her islands will not issue the *Licencia de Primera Ocupacion* (The Licence of First Occupation) without first seeing proof that the property has been registered. Of course, without the *Licencia de Primera Ocupacion* you will not be able to sign either the *Escritura* or obtain your electricity meter.

****

III   A Property that has recently been completed, but never lived in

Buying a new property that is already constructed, but as yet uninhabited, is the least complicated of the four options in this chapter. However, care must still be taken with regard to the drawing up of the Contract. The following should be included in the Contract of Sale & Purchase. Ensure that :

i.   A building licence has been issued for the property and details of the planning approval is reflected in the contract.

ii.   The certificates, from the Architect and the Town Hall, have been obtained for the completion of the building (*Certificado de fin de Obra*), the Licence of the first occupation (*Licencia de Primera Ocupacion*) and the *Boletin de Instalacion* (Certificate of Installation) issued by the *Delegacion de Industria* (Delegation of Industry) for the installation of the electricity and water. You will need copies of these Boletins to obtain your electric and water meters. The fact that the Developer/Builder has these documents, and that they have been paid, should be reflected in the Contract.

iii.   all the registration details must be included, the Finca number (the plot/land registration no.) the book no. etc. This information can be obtained from the *Escritura* (Deeds) or the *Nota Simple* (the Registration document from the Land Registry.

iv.   the total square meterage of the plot/land and the total constructed area of the property, plus terraces, should also be included.

v.   details of the Insurance policy have been included to ensure that if the Developer/Builder cannot complete the facilities on the complex, the insurance company will pay for their completion.

vi.   there are no connection charges for electricity, water or sewerage, and that you are only responsible for the payment of the installation of the electric meter and the water meter, if they are not already installed. The Developer/Builder should also supply you with the Gas Contract, to obtain the gas cylinders if gas appliances are installed.

vii. your quota of participation in the Community of Owners is clearly stated.

viii. the Developer/Builder is responsible for all debts on the property, up until the date of the signing of the *Escritura* and the handing over of the keys.

ix.   the price and payments to be made are clearly stated in the Contract.

x.   it is clearly stated in the Contract that you are only responsible for the costs of the *Escritura* for the Sale & Purchase of the property and not the segregation of the land or the declaration of the new building.

xi.   before signing the Contract, you ask to see a 'Nota Simple' proving that the person you are buying the property from is the registered legal owner of the property and that there are no mortgages or encumbrances on the property.

xii.   again, before signing the Contract, it makes sense to have some idea of the costs of the *Escritura* and the amount of *Plus Valia* Tax that you must pay, to ensure you don't have a nasty shock when you come to pay for it.

xiii.   you must ask to see proof that the annual *Contribuciones* and the community fees are paid up to date before making the final payment and signing the *Escritura*.

It is imperative that all payments are made to the Developer/ Builder through your Spanish Bank, as you will require a certificate from your Bank for the Notary, showing that the funds for the purchase of the property have been imported into Spain.

When you are buying a new property which is being built for you by the Developer/Builder, or any new property, it is very important when the building is completed that the Developer/Builder registers your property with the *RECAUDACION PROVINCIAL* (The Local Rates Office). This is also something that should be included in the Contract, as in many cases now, the Town Hall will insist on seeing proof that the property has been registered with the *RECAUDACION PROVINCIAL* before they will issue the *Licencia de Primera Ocupacion* (The Licence of First Occupation) which of course you will need to obtain both the *Escritura* (Deeds) for the property and the electric meter.

****

Note:
All the documents I have mentioned are most important, as without the Certificate of the termination of the building, you will not be able to make the *Escritura* for the declaration of the new building at the Notary's Office, and without the Licence of First

Occupation you will not be able to get an electricity meter connected to the property - and therefore no electricity supply.

The Certificate of the termination of the building is supplied by the architect, a copy of which is given to the Planning Department at the local Town Hall. This document informs the Planning authorities that the building has been finished, in accordance with the plans presented when the planning application was first made. The Planning Department then sends an Inspector to have a good look at the building to see if it agrees with these plans and they then issue the Licence of First Occupation. You should, of course, also receive copies of these documents. It should be clearly stated in the contract that the Developer/Builder is not only responsible for obtaining these documents, but is also responsible for their payment.

****

IV   *Buying a Plot of Land and Building your own Property*

If you are thinking of buying a plot of land and building your own house or villa, you must tread very carefully indeed. I would most certainly recommend you to use a lawyer, because the whole process is fraught with danger. Firstly, you must ensure that the local Town Hall will give you planning permission to build; if they say yes, how many square metres can you build? The agent, or person with whom you are negotiating to buy the land may, in all good faith, tell you that you can build a huge three or four bedroom villa with a double garage ..... but when you go for the planning approval, you find you can only build a small two bedroom house, with no garage - or you cannot build at all, because the land does not have the right specification for building on. To ensure that you will be able to build on the land that you are buying, you should obtain a document called an *Informe* from the Local Town Hall. This document would give you in writing exactly what the planning authorities will authorise you to build; the total square metres that can be built, and the height of the building.

Even after you have ascertained that you can build your dream house or villa, you still cannot relax - now you have to find an architect to do the project for the property and find a builder that has a good reputation. Finding an architect is not difficult, and he would no doubt help you with dealing with planning approval from the Town Hall. But be prepared to pay somewhere in the region of £3,000 - £5,000 for his fees. But beware! When you start building your house or villa and the Architect presents his fees, you will only be paying 70% of the total cost at this time - the other 30% becomes due when the building is finished, and the Certificate of the termination of the building, and the Licence of the first occupation of the property (as described earlier) are required. You need these two documents to be able to make the Declaration of the new building at the Notary's Office. Unfortunately, so often when people receive the first account from the architect they think that they have paid all his fees.

You must find a good builder, which is not always easy. In the UK, as you will know, there are many cowboy builders - so imagine how much more difficult it is going to be in a foreign country.

Once you have found a builder, a complete specification for the building work should be drawn up, reflecting for example the cost per square metre for tiles, the models and types of sanitary fittings, taps, doors, windows etc. and a completion date should be fixed, with a penalty clause for late completion (see point xii. on page 27). This document should be as such a contract between you and the builder, and should be signed by all parties concerned.

Even if, after all this, you still desperately want to build your own property, be prepared for the final cost of the building to be much greater than you first imagined it was going to be. This is always true, even when you are buying from a Developer/Builder, because there are always extra things that you want as the house or villa progresses under construction. If you request any alterations or additions to the property, you must always ask for a written quotation, and this should be signed by both parties, to save any disputes on 'extras' when the building is completed. Any major alterations or additions may also extend the completion date of the building. If this is the case, a new completion date should be agreed in writing and signed by both parties, as this will obviously affect the penalty clause for late completion in the Contract.

Before handing over the final payment for the land and signing the *Escritura*, ask to see proof that the annual *Contribuciones* are paid up to date.

When building a property on your own land, the electrician and plumber must obtain a *Boletin de Instalacion* (Certificate of Installation) from the *Delegacion de Industria* (Delegation of Industry) approving the installation, as you will need this certificate to obtain your electric and water meters. These certificates can only be obtained by registered electricians & plumbers, they must be members of the *Asociacion Provincial de Instaladores*.

To obtain your Escritura (Deeds) at the Notarys to make the *Decleracion de Obra Nueva* (Declaration of the New Building), apart from the building licence etc., you must register the new building with the *RECAUDACION PROVINCIAL* (The Rates Office). This is most important as many Town Halls in Spain now will not issue the *Licencia de Primera Ocupacion* (The Licence of First Occupation) without first seeing proof that the building has been registered. Your lawyer or architect will no doubt deal with this if you request it.

If you do go ahead and buy land and a Contract is drawn up for the purchase of the land, you should follow pretty much the instructions given in **Chapter 1**, dealing with buying a resale property, with regard to the documentation required and what should be included in the Contract. If you are buying land and building a property, then you will technically be making two *Escrituras*; at the time of paying the balance of the land price, you will make the *Escritura* for the land, and returning to the Notary's, to declare the new building on your land, once the property is completed. Please refer to **Chapter 4 *Escritura Costs*** to ascertain the total costs of making the *Escritura* for the land and later on for the costs of declaring the New Building.

* * *

CHAPTER 3

Buying a Property in the Country or an Inherited Property

This chapter will deal with buying a *Finca* (Farmland), *Cortijo* (farm-house) or a house in a Spanish village. If the *Finca* or village house is very old and has been handed down from generation to generation, it is quite probable that there is no *Escritura* for the property. Because these properties tend to be inherited through the family, usually no legal title deeds have ever been made. You have to tread very carefully when buying one of these. You will most definitely need the assistance of a Spanish lawyer.

When you are buying a *Finca*, you should be especially careful. There is a regulation that you can only build on a certain percentage of the square meterage of the land you are buying, and in some cases it may be impossible for you to build at all. If your idea is to alter or extend the existing property, or even demolish the existing structure and build a new house, you really must check with the local authorities exactly what you will be authorised to build. You will often find that at the most you will be able to renovate the existing building and not extend. As previously stated, you must use the services of a recommended lawyer when buying one of these types of property. He or she should be consulted before signing any contracts and handing over any deposits.

It is also important to have rights of way included in the *Escritura*, as well as water rights - water is normally supplied from a shared well in the countryside. I would also recommend a topographical survey and plan to be made of the land and its exact boundaries. It is quite customary for the owner of the land to tell you that the boundary is such and such an olive tree, and he might pick up a stone and throw it, saying that's roughly where the boundary is. That's all very well - but having a clearly marked boundary and plan could save future disputes erupting. It is also very important to reflect the exact square meterage of the *finca* in the contract of Sale & Purchase, as I have come across cases in the past where the purchaser was told that there were 5,000 square metres of land, which was not reflected in the contract - only to discover when the *Escritura* was signed that there were only 1,500 square metres of land.

As always, it makes good sense to be prepared.

You must also remove those rose-tinted spectacles when looking at farm properties, as it is not necessarily as idyllic as it may first appear. In the hilly and mountainous areas of Spain, farm properties are found up dirt tracks, very often a considerable distance from tarmaced roads, and when the rain comes in the winter - normally torrential, tropical-like rain storms - these tracks can become almost impassable and you would almost certainly need a four-wheel drive vehicle to get to and from the property. Very often there is no electricity supply to the property and, if it is possible to connect up to an electricity supply, this can prove very expensive. Also bear in mind that shops and facilities are not exactly on your doorstep, and what if someone is taken ill?! So, before embarking on buying a country property, do think very carefully.

As previously stated, it is quite probable that there is no title deed for the property that you are buying, but this is not to say that it is impossible to obtain a title deed. The normal procedure is that the lawyer must obtain what is called an *Expediente de Dominio*. Literally translated, it is proof of domination; in other words, a document to prove ownership. This particular document is issued by the Courts and not the Public Notary. I won't go into all the details of how this document is obtained, but basically a search has to be made to prove the ownership, an advice notice has to be placed in the *Boletin Oficial del Estado*, to give anybody who may have any claims on the property the chance to come forward. There are various other legalities, and it can take some considerable time to obtain this document - anything from a year to eighteen months and possibly longer. So it is necessary for your lawyer to retain a reasonable sum from the agreed price of the property until this document is available. Once you have the *Expediente de Dominio*, it is the same as having an *Escritura* for the property. This only applies of course when your lawyer has satisfied himself that the vendor/s can show sufficient proof that they are the legal owners.

It may well be suggested to you that you use the 205 Procedure to obtain the *Escritura* for the property. You can obtain an *Escritura* in a much shorter period of time with this document (Form 205) than you can with the *Expediente de Dominio* - the drawback being that for a period of 2 years from the date that your *Escritura* is registered at the Land Registry Office, somebody could claim ownership of the property. This is probably very unlikely to happen, as your lawyer would have checked all the relevant documents obtained from the present owners, proving ownership, and of course would have checked with the Land Registry Office to obtain a document called a *Certificado Negativo* (a Negative Certificate) showing that the Land Registry has searched their records and have found no registered owner of the property. However, it is a remote possibility and you should at least be aware of it. Your lawyer should explain both formats, the *Expediente de Dominio*, and the *205*, and advise which is the best way to obtain the *Escritura* for the property that you are buying.

In the case that the property you are buying has been inherited and the deceased owners had an *Escritura* and a Will leaving it to the vendors, you must ask to see proof that an *Escritura* has been made in the names of the vendors and see proof that any death duties due have been paid. This is most important, because if the property is still in the names of the deceased, how can you obtain an *Escritura* in your name? Plus, of course, there are the problems that you could inherit with regard to death duties. Again, my advice in these cases is to consult a Spanish lawyer.

As far as the contracts are concerned for the purchase of a country or inherited property, you should follow very much the procedures explained in **Chapter 1 Buying a Resale Property**.

CHAPTER 4

Escritura Costs

The costs for an *Escritura* vary, naturally, according to the value of the property you are buying and what you are declaring the price to be - which is of course the price to be shown on the *Escritura*.

It is the custom in Spain to under-declare the value of the property that you are buying, and in the past it was common to declare about 30% of the value. However, the tax authorities are now valuing the properties at much higher levels, and although you will be asked to under-declare the value of the property, as a rule of thumb, you shouldn't declare less than 75 - 80% of the price that you are paying and of course declare the actual value if you can. It is always a good idea to consult with your lawyer or the Notary's Office with regard to the minimum that should be declared on the *Escritura* to avoid any supplementary charges being made, as explained below.

The authorities will compare the value you have declared on your *Escritura* against their tables of values for properties in your area, and if they find that your declared value is lower than their valuation, they can demand a supplementary charge of 6% on the difference, plus administration charges and postage. In the case that the difference in your declared value is 20% or 2.000.000 Ptas/€12.020.24 centimos less than their valuation, they can charge you in the region of 20% of the difference.

As an example, a property in Malaga was declared at a value of 7.500.000 Ptas/€45.075.91c. and the *Junta de Andalucia* inspected the property and valued it at 13.500.000 Ptas/€81.136.63c.

The fine imposed was 1.200.000 Ptas/€7.212.15c. (approximately £4,800). Had the correct amount been declared in the first place, the total cost for the difference would have been 420.000 Ptas/ €2.524.25c. (approximately £1,680). If the declared value is 50% less than the official valuation, you can be obligated to sell the property to the authorities for the declared value. As far as I know, this has never happened, but it pays to check with your lawyer or the Notary's Office as to what the lowest value to be declared should be, to avoid any supplementary charges - if you are in agreement with declaring a lower value.

As a rule of thumb, on a resale property, you need to allow approximately 9% of the total price of the property as being the costs of the *Escritura*. On a property that is being built for you, these costs of course can be greatly increased if you are having to pay the *Escritura* for the purchase of the land, the segregation of your land from the rest of the *urbanizacion*, and the declaration of the new building, as stated in the previous chapter dealing with the purchase of a new property.

The costs of an *Escritura of Compra/Venta*, depending on the category of property being purchased, are broken down as follows :

1.   Resale Property

•   Transfer Tax of 6% of the declared value of the property.

•   Notary's fees for preparing the *Escritura* and legalising the document, of which there is a scale of charges, according to the declared value of the property and the number of pages in the *Escritura*.

•   A deposit for the land registry office of approximately 0.5% of the declared value.

Plus Valia is a local Council tax which is assessed on the increase of the value of the land since the previous owner bought the property and subsequently sold it to you. Therefore the longer the people you are buying from have owned the property, the greater this tax will be. Thus, it is a good idea to ascertain the *Plus Valia* Tax before you sign the Contract and pay a deposit on the property. In fact, as I have said so often before, it is not a bad idea to know the total costs of the *Escritura* before you sign and pay the deposit.

The law in Spain states that the person selling the property should pay the *Plus Valia* tax, but in reality it has become the custom in Spain that the Purchaser pays all the costs, including the *Plus Valia*. You obviously only pay this tax once - when you sell, the person buying from you pays this tax. The reason it has become the custom for the Purchaser to pay is this: if the Vendor is a foreigner and, after selling, that person returns to their country of origin - should the tax remain unpaid, it will probably fall back onto the person who bought the property. Under recent new legislation, the local Town Hall can now go against the property purchased if the *Plus Valia* is not paid, even if it was previously agreed that the Vendor would pay this. Therefore, if it is agreed at the contract stage of the purchase that the Vendor will pay the *Plus Valia*, this amount should be deducted from the final payment, to ensure that the Vendor actually pays this. Your lawyer or estate agent can obtain the amount that the *Plus Valia* will be from the local Town Hall and advise you before signing the contracts.

2.   New Property

When you are buying a property from a Developer/Builder which is to be built for you from plans, a property under construction or a new property which is finished but has never been inhabited :

- IVA TAX (VAT) at 7% of the declared value of the property is paid to the Developer/Builder prior to the signing of the *Escritura*. The exception is in the Canary Islands, where the IVA Tax (VAT) is only 4.5%.

- Stamp duty of 0.5% on the declared value of the property.

- A deposit for the land registry office of approximately 0.5% of the declared value of the property.

- *Plus Valia* Tax as detailed above.

In this category, you will find that the total *Escritura* costs are 1.5% more than when buying a resale property. The above figures also apply to garages situated in the same place as the dwelling and purchased on the same date.

Please note:

If the garage you are buying is in a different place, or is purchased on a different day, you pay 16% IVA Tax (VAT) and not 7% as previously stated. Otherwise the figures are as detailed above.

The 16% IVA Tax (VAT) also applies to commercial premises.

If you have not previously agreed in the Contract of Sale & Purchase that the Developer/Builder is responsible for the costs of the segregation; declaration of the new building; or the Horizontal division, in the case of an apartment block, your costs will be much higher. So it is very important that this has been made clear at the time of drawing up and signing the Contract of Sale & Purchase.

3.   Buying a Plot of Land and Building your own Property

In this category, the *Escritura* costs are greater because you will be technically making two *Escrituras* - one for the land and, later, another for the new building.

- Transfer Tax of 6% of the declared value of the land.

- A deposit for the land registry office of approximately 0.5% of the declared value of the land.

- *Plus Valia* Tax as previously detailed in this chapter.

Once the villa you are building is completed, you must return to the Notary's Office to make the declaration of the new building. The costs for this *Escritura* are as follows :

- Stamp Duty of 0.5% on the declared value of the new building.

- Notary's fees for preparing and legalising the document, of which there is a scale of charges, according to the declared value of the building.

- A deposit for the land registry office of approximately 0.5% of the declared value.

As a bonus under this category, please note that there is no *Plus Valia* Tax on the declaration of a new building.

After signing the *Escritura*, you normally have 30 days to pay all these costs. If the costs are not paid within this time limit, there is normally a fine of 10% on the amount outstanding up to three months after the date of signing. Once three months have elapsed, the fine increases to 50%, so beware!

To save yourself a lot of running around, it is a good idea to deposit the funds for the costs of the *Escritura* with your lawyer or the agent you are buying your property from and they will pay these accounts on your behalf and should obviously give you an account and receipts of payment. If the agent who you are buying the property from does this for you, he should not ask for any payment for doing so - this is all part of his responsibility, and is part of what he is receiving commission for on the sale of the property to you. The only things he will charge you for is obtaining your Certificate of *No Residente* in Spain, at the time of buying property in Spain; and your *N.I.E.* number (see below). There is in fact a charge made by the Ministry of the Interior for this certificate, and there is also a charge for dealing with the payment of the 5% retention. If it applies, it must be deposited at the local tax office. There will also be a charge of approximately 5.000 Ptas/€30.05c. to transfer the electricity contract to your name. The amount charged is determined by the Kws that have been contracted.

The estate agent that you are buying the property from should, in my opinion, also go with you to the local electricity board to deal with the change of name on the electricity contract. He/she should also arrange the change of name with the Administrator of the Community; the Local Authorities for the annual rates (commonly known as *Contribuciones*); and the water board if applicable. This is something I have always done for my clients and there should, of course, be no charge made for this service - as I have already stated, this is part of the work that *should* be done for you, and represents a portion of the commission estate agents receive. There is, however, one exception - the transfer of the telephone to your name. This has to be dealt with in the capital of the Province, and could be a good distance from where you are buying your property.

All these necessary tasks are, I am sure, things you would find most difficult to do, as most people buying in Spain do not speak Spanish and, being in an 'alien' environment, do not know the procedures. So it is good to know that help *should* be to hand.

In the case of a new property that hasn't been lived in or a property that has been built for you, the estate agent (again!) should assist you with arranging the installation of the electric meter and contracting the supply of electricity with the local electricity board. Also, he should register your name with the Administrator of the Community, and the local rates office to enable you to pay your annual *contribuciones*. Under normal circumstances, the builder will install the water meter for you.

Under recent legislation, foreign people who are buying a property in Spain must now obtain a *Certificado de No Residente en España*, which is obtained through the local national police station. You must present your passport or a notarised photocopy of your passport, along with a form with details of your full name, date of birth, etc. At the same time, and with the same form, it is a good idea to apply for your N.I.E. number, *Numero Identification Extranjero*, which literally translated is Number of Identification as a Foreigner. The Notary's Office needs your N.I.E. number for the *Escritura*. You will also need it to insure your property and its contents. You need this number to register you with the Spanish tax authorities, as you will have to pay certain taxes on the property you are buying. These taxes are explained in greater detail in the chapter dealing with tax obligations in Spain.

CHAPTER 5

Community of Owners

In England, local Councils are responsible for the upkeep of roads, green areas, and street lighting on an estate or around an apartment block. In Spain, the apartment block or *urbanizacion* is completely private to the owners and it is therefore the responsibility of the owners themselves to deal with the upkeep. Thus, a community of owners is formed, and each owner is obliged to pay proportionately towards the costs involved.

The *Comunidad de Propietarios* (Community of Owners) is composed of all the owners of villas, apartments and business premises in the development complex. They are responsible for the payment of the maintenance of zones of common ownership, and this also includes areas like hallways and communal gardens. The payment of taxes and other expenses is attributable to the complex as a whole, as well as the promotion of harmony among its members.

An *Administrador de Fincas* (Administrator of Properties) is appointed by the community of owners to deal with the aforementioned payments and he/she prepares annual accounts for the community meetings, which are held annually. The amount each owner will have to pay in community fees is set according to the quota of participation in the community and the services that are included. Your quota is stated in the *Escritura*, so you can easily check if the amount of participation is correct when assessing your community fees. Some communities include the exterior painting of the apartment block or all the villas/houses on the complex every 2/3 years, so the community fees would be higher than on a complex where this is not included. At the AGM (Annual General Meeting), of which the owners should be informed well in advance, a President, Treasurer and Secretary will be elected by the owners. Whoever is elected must, of course, be one of the owners. You can also change or reappoint the Administrator as the case may be at this meeting. Additionally, complaints and suggestions can be put forward at the AGM and voted on accordingly.

It is very important for all owners to make an effort to attend the AGM, because all decisions taken at these meetings will affect each owner on that particular complex. If you are unable to attend, you should give somebody your proxy to vote on your behalf at the meeting. It is very important that all owners keep their community payments up to date, as failure to pay can result in your property being embargoed by the community of owners, and the subsequent auctioning of the property to recover the outstanding debt.

The payment of the community fees can vary tremendously. You may find the community of the complex where you are buying your property requests payments half-yearly, or you may have to pay the whole year in advance. The most sensible thing to do, if you are not residing permanently in Spain, is to make a standing order with your Spanish Bank to make these payments on your behalf. It is also a good idea to find out when these payments are to be made, so that you ensure you have enough cover in the account.

You should, of course, also ascertain what the annual community fees are before you sign the contracts, so you have an idea of what your annual outgoings are going to be. As I have explained earlier in the book, some community fees can be high and you don't want any nasty surprises after you have bought your property. It's a good idea to obtain a copy of the statutes of the community, so you know the rules and regulations that govern the community you will be joining.

Bear in mind that the rules and regulations of communities are binding on all members. If for example you are planning to live permanently in Spain and you have a dog, but the community rules do not allow pets, it would be quite a problem if you had bought not knowing this, so you can see obtaining a copy of the statutes is very important. Your estate agent or lawyer should be able to help you with regard to obtaining copies of the community statutes.

CHAPTER 6

Power of Attorney

A Power of Attorney will be required if you are not able to travel to Spain to sign the *Escritura*; or, if you are a couple, one of you cannot be there and you want the *Escritura* made out in both your names.

As far as making a Power of Attorney is concerned, it makes sense for you to arrange this while you are in Spain - when you are signing the contracts, for example. To make a Power of Attorney in the UK works out a lot more expensive than preparing it in Spain, and it is a lot more complicated.

To make a Power of Attorney in Spain, you simply go along to the local Notary's Office, giving him your personal details along with your passport details and what you want the Power of Attorney *for*, and to whom you are giving the Power of Attorney *to*. The cost of a Special Power of Attorney is 7.100 Ptas/€42.67c. A Special Power of Attorney will only authorise the person to whom you've given the Power of Attorney to buy or sell a specified property for you, nothing more. If you make a General Power of Attorney (the cost of which is approximately 9.000 Ptas/€54.09c.) this authorises the person to whom you've given the Power of Attorney to do almost anything on your behalf - for example, buy or sell property, apply for loans, obtain a mortgage.

In my opinion, in the majority of cases, it is sufficient to make a Special Power of Attorney.

If for any reason you do not have time to have this prepared while you are in Spain, you will need a solicitor who is authorised to make a Power of Attorney in the Spanish language, and it must, to be legal in Spain, have an *Apostille*, which authenticates the document. So, if you are having to make the Power of Attorney in England, the best plan is to get in touch with the nearest Spanish Consulate to request a list of solicitors who are authorised to prepare a Power of Attorney for Spain. The cost of preparing the document this way is at least double what you would expect to pay in Spain, and as I have already pointed out, much more involved. Thus, it does make sense to try to have the document prepared while you are actually in Spain.

If you decide to make the Power of Attorney at the Spanish Consulate (which of course is possible) there is NO need for an *Apostille*. When you sign the Power of Attorney in the Spanish Consulate, it is regarded as the same as if you had signed the document in Spain.

CHAPTER 7

Making a Spanish Will

It is always sensible to make a last Will & Testament and, if you are buying a property in Spain and you would like peace of mind, I would say that it is imperative. Under Spanish law, property automatically passes from husband to wife, or wife to husband, as the case may be. Property then passes to any children on the death of both. If you don't make a last Will & Testament in Spain, it could mean that it has to go to Probate, as your own country's laws of Inheritance would apply. So, to save any complications, it makes very good sense to make a Will in Spain when you are buying your property there.

The estate agent, or lawyer, that you are dealing with will be able to arrange the Will(s) to be signed at the same time as you are signing the *Escritura*. Under recent new Spanish legislation, Wills are now prepared in two columns: one column in Spanish and the second column in your own language. Theoretically, the translation of the Will into English, for example, should be translated by an official translator, but generally speaking the Notary will accept a translation being made by someone who is known to have a good command of both languages.

If you are buying in joint names, you both need to make a Will. Each Will is going to cost approximately 25.000 Ptas/€150.25c. The reason for the comparatively high cost is because of the translation that has to be made; also the Notary's fees for preparing the Wills and presiding over the signing, as well as legalising them.

After the signing of the Wills, you are given a *copia simple* (a copy of the original) minus signatures. The original signed copy remains in the Notary's Office. The Notary's Office then sends a document of registration to the central registration office in Madrid, with just the details of the number of the Wills, the date they were signed, at what time they were signed, and giving your names. No details of the contents of your Wills are given. If one or both of the owners should die, the surviving partner or the children need to obtain a Death Certificate, with an official translation into Spanish, which must have an *Apostille*. This is not difficult to obtain, so it is not something that you should worry about.

On obtaining the Death Certificate and the official translation with the *Apostille*, these should be presented, along with a copy of the Will, either to a *Gestoria*, or your lawyer, who will deal with the inheritance for you. They will contact the Notary's Office, for them to request a certificate from the Central Register in Madrid, advising of the last Will & Testament registered with them. On receipt of this certificate, the Notary will be able to make a new *Escritura* in the name(s) of the person(s) inheriting the property.

You have a maximum period of six months to present the necessary documents to the tax authorities and you will of course have to pay death duties on the inheritance. The amount you will have to pay and the discounts allowed are complex, as are the inheritance taxes that are applied. Just to give you a rough idea, if you are over 21 years of age at the time of inheriting property in Spain, you will be allowed to inherit the sum per person of 2.655.000 Ptas/€15.956.87. free of tax; you will also be allowed to deduct the costs of funeral expenses and any costs incurred for medical attention prior to the death of the person concerned. In the case of children inheriting property, who at the time of his/her parent's death were under 21 years of age, the amount that can be inherited free of tax is 2.655.000 Ptas/€15.956.87c. plus 664.00 Ptas/ €3.990.72c. for each year under the age of 21, plus any discounts. As an example, if a child was 17 at the time of the death of his/her parents, the discount allowed would be 2.655.000 Ptas/ €15.956.87c., plus 4 x 664.00 Ptas/€3.990.72c., which gives a total of 5.311.000 Ptas/€31.919.75c. The maximum amount allowed is 7.963.000 Ptas/€47.858.59c.

The percentage of tax payable on the taxable balance is on a complicated scale, which ranges from 7.65% to 34.00%. To ascertain what death duties would apply, the best thing to do is to consult either your Lawyer or *Gestoria*.

On top of the Lawyer's/*Gestoria*'s fees, you will have the costs of making a new *Escritura* for the property in question.

One way of avoiding death duties is to put the property you are buying in the names of your children, because according to the law of averages, children should outlive their parents. You can also put a clause in the *Escritura* that your children cannot sell the property without your consent and cannot refuse you access to the property as long as you live. If you do decide to buy the property in your children's names, it does mean of course that their names should be on the contract, and that they would have to travel to Spain to sign the *Escritura*, or give someone the Power of Attorney to do so on their behalf.

If the *Escritura* is going to be in the children's names, the costs of the *Escritura* are the same. However, if you are retaining the right to use the property until your death, and that your children cannot sell the property without your consent, it will increase the costs of the *Escritura* - so before proceeding, do ascertain the extra cost involved.

Once you have made a Will & Testament in Spain, there is no need to make another Will should you sell one property and then buy another. This is because when you make a Will & Testament in Spain, it states that this Will covers anything you own in Spain at the time of death, for example property, stocks & shares.

Also, as previously stated, the Will & Testament is normally made leaving property to a husband/wife, and on the death of both, to any children, and on the death of the children, to grandchildren. Therefore the only time you will need to draw up a new Will & Testament is if you wish to alter the beneficiaries or what they will inherit.

CHAPTER 8

Residencia and Work Permits

If you are planning to go to live in Spain permanently, you must obtain *Residencia* there. A *Residencia* does not affect your nationality and you still retain your British Passport.

The advantages of taking up *Residencia* in Spain far outweigh the disadvantages, and it is an obligation if you are planning to live in Spain for more than 183 days a year. If you qualify for an E121, you can be registered with the Spanish health authorities and receive free health care under the Spanish Social Security system. If you are a pensioner you will also receive other benefits, such as reduced fares on public transport, and of course you will not be liable for tax on your property, as would be the case if you were a non resident.

The procedure to obtain your *Residencia* in Spain is now comparatively simple for member countries of the European Community. There are, however, certain documents that you will need to obtain in the UK before you go to live in Spain, which I detail as follows :

• You will need to write to the DSS in Newcastle to ask if you qualify for an E121. In the past, to qualify for this form you needed to have been paying your National Insurance stamps for a given period; however, it would seem that according with recent EU regulations, you must now be of retirement age to obtain this document. To ascertain if you qualify, you will need to give them your NHS number, letting them know that you are taking up permanent residence in Spain. They will also need to know your new address in Spain.

If you are going to stay in Spain for a reasonable length of time, but do not intend taking up *Residencia*, you can obtain an E111 from a general Post Office. This will give you medical cover in Spain for a limited period, which I believe is up to a year. However, do enquire how long the cover is when you obtain the E111. Under normal circumstances you will not be able to obtain *Residencia* in Spain with an E111.

To obtain your *Residencia* once you have arrived, you need the following documents :

Certificate of Registration with the Seguridad Social

Take your E121 along to the nearest offices of the *Seguridad Social* (Social Security), which is normally attached to one of the *Ambulatorios*, and register yourself with the Spanish Health Service. They will give you a certificate of your registration, which you will need to apply for your *Residencia*.

If you do not qualify for an E121, to obtain your *Residencia* you will need to take out a private health insurance. There are several Spanish health insurances available and of course it must cover all aspects of health care, to include doctors, hospitalisation, etc. To give you some idea of the cost of private health cover in Spain, I asked a local broker to give me an idea of the amount per month/year, and they gave me a figure of 6.600 Ptas/€39.67 centimos per month, which is 79.200Ptas/€476.04 centimos per annum, these figures being per person. This equates to £26.40p. per month or £316.80 per annum at an exchange rate of 250 Pesetas to the £. Of course if you are 65 or over, the cost would increase to 9.200 Ptas/€55.29 centimos per month, 110.400 Ptas/€663.48 centimos per annum, which equates to £36.80p. per month or £441.60p. per annum, again using the exchange rate of 250 Pesetas to the £. As from 1st March 2002 the exchange rate will be exclusively against the Euro, as the Peseta will cease being legal currency from this date.

If you presently have private health cover in the UK, do check to see if the policy can be adapted to cover you in Spain. However, you will need a certificate, in the Spanish language, proving that your existing policy does in fact cover you for full health care in Spain. This of course does not apply if you are going to be working in Spain, as you will be paying Social Security. For this category, please refer to the section headed **Residencia/Work Permit as an Employee or Self Employed Person.**

Certificate of Income

You will need a certificate from your Spanish Bank showing that you have had an average balance of 75.000 Ptas/€450.76c. a month per person. This is the amount that the Spanish Authorities have set as being the amount required for you to live on in Spain. The certificate normally states that you have had an average balance in your account of at least this amount a month, per person, over a period of six months.

This does not mean that you need to pay in 75.000 Ptas/€450.76c. for each of you (assuming you are a couple) every month, for a period of six months - if you transferred into your Spanish Bank account the sum of 1.000.000 Ptas/€6.010.12c in, say, April, to cover the costs of the *Escritura* (Deeds) and any other expenses, and you applied for the certificate, for example, in June - your average balance over a six month period would be 166.666 Ptas/€1.001.68c.

per month, which give you each the sum of 83.333 Ptas/€500.84c. per month, which of course is more than the minimum required.

Once you have obtained the Certificate of Registration with the Social Security in Spain, or you have the policy for private health care in Spain, plus the Certificate from your Spanish Bank, you are almost ready to go along to the nearest National Police Station. You will need the *Extranjeros* Department (Foreigners Department) which deals with applications for *Residencia*. You will also need the following:

- Your passport(s) and two photocopies of each. (If you still have the old dark-blue-fronted passports, you will need to present two photocopies of each page, up to and including the date of issue page.) If you have the new European Union Passport, you need only present two photocopies of the last page (the one containing your photograph).

- Four passport-size photographs.

- Certificate of registration with the *Seguridad Social, or* a certificate of private health cover in Spain, plus two photocopies.

- Bank Certificate proving income, plus two photocopies.

You will need to fill in a form at the department dealing with *Residencia* applications and at the same time present all your accumulated documents. They will take impressions of your fingerprints, on both the *Residencia* card and on the application forms, and will probably advise you that you must return for your *Residencia* in approximately three months. As it does take some time for it to come through, it's not a bad idea to carry your copy of the application form with you, should you need it for any reason.

The estate agent you are dealing with will be able to advise you on where you need to go on your *Residencia* quest, but if you feel this is too complicated for you to deal with on your own, I would advise you to go along to a recommended *Gestoria*, who will deal with it all for you. It isn't too difficult. By dealing with it yourself you will save a reasonable sum of money and, if you are a couple - or if you are with friends - you could spoil yourselves with a slap-up meal and a few bottles of wine, to celebrate.

Your Residence Card will be valid for five years. The renewal of the card should be applied for in the local Police Station just before the current card expires, and you will need to present the same documentation as you did on the previous application.

If you are planning to work in Spain, you will require a *Residencia*/work permit. This type of Resident's permit is different to a normal *Residencia* in the sense that you do not need to prove any income, but of course you must either have a contract of employment or, if you are self-employed, you must be registered with the Tax authorities. My advice would be to get a *Gestoria* to deal with your application for the *Residencia*/work permit, as it could prove complicated for you, particularly if you do not speak Spanish.

The procedures for obtaining a *Residencia*/work permit as an employee or as a self-employed person are as follows :

Work Permit as an Employee

You need to go to the local INEM office to register as available for employment. The INEM office is the employment office in Spain. On telling them that you have been offered employment, they will issue you with a card, which will be necessary for you to obtain a *Residencia*/work permit.

You must present the card issued by the INEM office to your employer or his *Gestoria*. They will also need your registration card with the Social Security in Spain to prepare your contract of employment.

Your employer must give you a copy of the contract that you have both signed, detailing all the terms and conditions of employment. This must be presented to the *Gestoria* who is dealing with the application for your *Residencia*/work permit, along with two photocopies and the following documents :

- Your passport(s) and two photocopies. If you are still using the old dark blue-fronted passports, you will need to present two photocopies of each page, up to and including the Date of Issue page. If you have the new European Union Passport, you need only two photocopies of the last page (the one containing your photograph).

- Four passport-size photographs

- The certificate with your N.I.E. number, plus two photocopies, if you already have it. If you haven't applied for your N.I.E. number, this can be applied for at the same time as you make your application for *Residencia*.

- Proof of registration with the Social Security in Spain. The obvious evidence of this is your Social Security card, which shows your Social Security number. Again, you will need two photocopies.

The company or person who is employing you should help you with registering with the Social Security and you will receive a registration card showing your Social Security number. It will also show you the name of the doctor you have been registered with.

Work Permit as a Self-employed Person

Once you have found the premises for your business, you must obtain an Opening Licence from the local Town Hall. To obtain this you need detailed plans drawn up by an *Ingeniero Tecnico Industrial* (Industrial Technical Engineer) and they must be stamped and approved by the *Colegio Oficial de Ingenieros Industriales* (The Official College of Industrial Technical Engineers). You must then present them to the Town Hall and pay for the licence. You must also obtain a Fiscal Licence, and register with the Social Security to obtain a Social Security number.

If your business involves the handling of food, i.e. you are going to open a restaurant or something similar, you must sit an examination on all the do's and don'ts of dealing with food, which does seem a sensible idea. It is not difficult, and you will receive a certificate for your efforts. You must obtain this document before you can get your *Residencia*/Work Permit.

You must also produce the *Escritura* or rental contract for the premises you are running your business from, plus two photocopies; your passport and two photocopies, and four passport photographs. (If you are presenting a rental contract, this must have been registered with the *Camara de la Propiedad* (Registry of Rented Properties) and stamped as registered.)

You will also need :

- *Licencia Fiscal* (Fiscal Licence - Tax Licence) obtainable from the local tax office

- *Alta Autonomos* (you must register with the Social Security office in Spain) obtainable from the local Social Security office

- *Licencia de Aperatura* (Opening Licence) obtainable from the local Town Hall

There is, of course, nothing to stop you doing this yourself, but as I have said previously, it is complicated, and if you only have a limited knowledge of Spanish, or none at all, it is almost impossible. Therefore, as previously suggested, I would advise that you get a *Gestoria* to deal with it for you. In fact you will need a *Gestoria* to deal with such things as the payments of Social Security, taxes, IVA (VAT) when you have your business up and running.

If you are buying what is classed as a leasehold business, tread very carefully, because to all intents and purposes leases no longer exist in Spain. It is realistically now a rental contract for 5 years.

You can be asked high prices for premises which - it is claimed - have a long term lease, which due to changes in Spanish law regarding leasehold property, only have a five year rental contract now. Therefore, before committing yourself to the purchase of what is categorised as a leasehold property, do consult a lawyer. If, for example, it turns out that the property only has a rental contract for five years, all you should be paying for is any building work which was carried out and fixtures & fittings. With regard to the rent that you are paying, this can only be upped by the official increase in the cost of living index, which is published by the Government every year. When you are negotiating the contract of rental, it is not a bad idea to see if you can reach agreement on a renewal of the contract at the end of the five years over which you are currently renting the property. You will also find that the owner will want a clause in the contract stating that he will receive anything between 10% and 30% of the price that you sell the lease/rental contract on for. This is something your lawyer should negotiate with the owner on your behalf.

Another thing that your lawyer should check out for you is the opening licence, which is obtained from the local Town Hall. I have come across cases, for example, where the premises only have an opening licence for a supermarket, and the present owners have converted the premises into a bar and sold the freehold or lease at a reasonably low price; the person who bought it discovers that the local Town Hall would only authorise an opening licence for a supermarket and nothing else.

Under recent new legislation, you are now obliged to retain 18% of the rental paid to the landlord/owner of the property from where you are running your business. The amount retained of course is for the Tax Authorities and I would assume the reason that this measure has been introduced is because many landlords/owners were not declaring this rental income.

If you are buying the freehold on a business property, the documentation and the clauses in the contracts should be pretty much the same as stated in **Chapter 1 Buying a Resale Property**. However, you would be well advised to use the services of a recommended lawyer to deal with the contracts and to ensure that the premises have the correct licences for the business.

CHAPTER 9

Spanish Driving Licences

If you are planning to drive while you are in Spain, you will obviously need to take your British driving licence with you. You do not need an International licence. However, if you decide you would be happier having an International driving licence, these are readily available from your local AA office.

If you are going to live in Spain permanently and you are going to apply for *Residencia*, under recent EU regulations you should no longer need to exchange your UK driving licence for a Spanish licence. However, my advice is to still obtain a Spanish driving licence, because the Spanish Police could give you some hassle - the Spanish driving licence bears your photograph and, as you know (unless you have one of the new driving licences) your UK one doesn't. If you have residential status in Spain, as far as the authorities are concerned you have the same standing as a Spanish citizen, so you should therefore have a Spanish driving licence. It's really in your own interests.

To obtain your Spanish licence, you have to hand in your British licence, which you will find is not returned to you. Your British licence is retained by the authorities on issue of the Spanish licence because, as mentioned, as far as they are concerned you are now regarded as a Spanish citizen and have no further need of the British equivalent, the logic being that your permanent residence is now in Spain.

You will need to have a medical examination, which is quite straightforward, and it must be carried out by an approved medical centre in Spain. You will also need three passport size photographs, one of which is attached to the medical certificate, one to the Spanish driving licence, and the third retained on the authority's files.

Once you have all the necessary documents, they should be presented to the Provincial traffic authorities, which normally have their offices in the capital city of that province. For example, in the case of Malaga Province, the offices are in Malaga.

To reiterate, the documentation required is :

- The original and a photocopy of your *Residencia* card

- Medical certificate

- Your British driving licence

- Three passport size photographs

When you apply for your Spanish driving licence, you could of course undertake this task yourself, but my advice would be to either ask your lawyer to deal with it for you, or alternatively approach a *Gestoria*, because the time, and possible complications you may have trying to communicate with the Spanish authorities, really may not be worth your while.

Renewal of Driving Licence

- From 18 to 40 years old, the licence will be renewed every 10 years

- From 40 to 45 years old, it will be renewed from 10 to 15 years according to your age

- From 45 to 66 years old, it will be renewed every 5 years

- From 66 to 70 years old, the licence will be renewed every 1-5 years according to your age

- From 70 years old, it will be renewed every year

The renewal of a driving licence can be made through the post office presenting the necessary documents and paying 2.200 Ptas/€13.22c. in respect of *Tráfico*'s (Traffic Department's) charges.

General Obligations for Drivers

Private cars may not travel faster than 50 kilometres per hour in urban areas and 120 km/h maximum on motorways and dual-carriageways.

It is obligatory to have:

- A driving licence

- Valid third party insurance. Spanish Insurance Companies will not insure foreign registered vehicles

- Original identification documents of the vehicle: technical inspection card and traffic permit (Photocopies are only admissible if they are certified by a Notary, at a cost of 500 Ptas/€3.00c. per page; the Municipal Police, *Tráfico* or some Banks)

Also it is obligatory to always wear a safety belt in a car, and a crash helmet when on a motorbike or moped.

If you commit some breach of traffic regulations outside the urban area and you get a fine, you will have a 20% discount if you pay the fine within 10 days. Serious fines do not qualify. The payments will be made in the *Tráfico* offices, usually in the main town of the province.

CHAPTER 10

Mortgages

It may be that you'll find in Spain your ideal, absolutely one hundred per cent perfect property - but, alas, you don't have the extra cash that you would need to go ahead and buy it. You're sure you wont be able to find another property quite as marvellous, and you're wondering what you can do, short of selling your car, and Great Aunt Mabel's antique jewellery. Before you take such drastic steps, you might like to consider the possibility of taking out a mortgage on the property, to make up the shortfall.

As interest rates in Spain are currently very low, you could apply to a Spanish bank for a mortgage, the only drawback being that you would be repaying the mortgage in Pesetas/Euros and therefore subject to a fluctuating exchange rate. You may therefore prefer to obtain a mortgage in Pounds Sterling. If this is the case, you could contact the Abbey National in Gibraltar. The Abbey National can offer mortgages to UK residents, EU Nationals, and non-EU Nationals who have resided in the UK for a minimum of 10 years. The Abbey National (Gibraltar) Ltd is a wholly owned subsidiary of Abbey National Plc and may be prepared to give you a mortgage of up to 75% of the valuation of the property - subject of course to status - over a period of 25 years. The minimum period is 5 years and the minimum amount they can lend is £25,000. (Please refer to **Minimum Loan** later in this chapter.) If the property is valued at less than £50,000 the amount lent is reduced to 60%.

If you are buying in the Balearic or Canary Islands (Mallorca, Menorca, or Tenerife, Lanzarote etc.) the ***Banca March*** specialise in mortgages on these Islands, where they have branches of their bank as well as in London. They offer a maximum lending facility of 60% of the valuation of the property and will lend in both Pounds Sterling and Pesetas/Euros. Please refer to Page 85 for more information.

Mortgages - Abbey National

The mortgage is, naturally, repaid in Sterling, which saves you having to worry about fluctuating exchanges. The interest rate is currently 1.95% over the base rate in the UK.

Quite a number of clients of mine have arranged mortgages with the Abbey National in Gibraltar, and all have been very satisfied with the professional and efficient service they have received.

You can contact the Abbey National at the following address :

Abbey National (Gibraltar) Ltd
237 Main Street
Gibraltar

Telephone: 00 350 76090
Telex: 2158 Abbey GK
Fax::   00 350 72028

The following is a more complete explanation of the lending policy for the Abbey National in Gibraltar :

Lending Areas

Spain
The coastal strip of southern Spain including the Costa del Sol, Costa Blanca, Costa Brava and Costa de la Luz, together with the Balearic Islands. All large towns will be considered by management on an individual case basis.

Portugal
The Algarve, Lisbon area and Madeira.

Currency
Sterling

Eligibility
All EU Nationals (residing in their home country or in the UK) except in Spain to holders of Spanish *Residencia* and Portugal to Portuguese Nationals.

Non EU Nationals permanently resident in the UK for a minimum qualifying period of 10 years - subject to management approval on an individual case basis.

Minimum Loan : Portugal and Spain
£25,000

Maximum Loan
£450,000 (subject to Board approval)

Term
5 - 25 years

Repayment Method
Repayment (repayments of interest and capital) or Endowment (repayments of interest only with a suitable Endowment Policy in force)

Life Assurance
Life assurance is required for the duration of the mortgage, and existing policies may be utilised.

Multiple Loan

Restricted to one mortgage per applicant

Method of Purchase

Spain

Advances to individuals or though non-trading Gibraltar, Jersey, Guernsey, Isle of Man, and British Virgin Islands off-shore companies.

Portugal

Advances to non-trading Gibraltar, Jersey, Guernsey and Isle of Man offshore companies.

Security

Spain

First charge over the Spanish property. If the advance is through a company a charge is secured over the shares of the company.

Portugal

A charge is secured over the shares of the company.

Status Requirements

For individual mortgages - 3 times your guaranteed annual income plus 1 times all secondary income; however, the amount you can borrow may be reduced if you have any continuing mortgage or other credit agreements.

For joint mortgages - either:

BASIS 1: 3 times the guaranteed annual income of the main income earner, plus 1 times the principal income of one other applicant, plus 1 times all secondary income; however, the amount you can borrow may be reduced if you have any continuing mortgage or other credit agreements OR

BASIS 2: 2 ½ times your joint guaranteed annual income, plus 1 times all secondary income; however, the amount you can borrow may be reduced if you have any continuing mortgage or other credit agreements.

Submission and approval

- Certified passport copy

- 6 months personal bank statements showing salary credits

- Latest P60 or tax assessment

- Proof of deposit

- Latest mortgage statement

- 2 documents for proof of address, e.g. utility bill

- 3 years cerftified accounts if self-employed

Applications are not accepted from self-employed/company directors who are non-UK nationals.

Percentage Advance - both purchase and remortgage facilities

Portugal and Spain
75%* All UK Nationals irrespective of country of residence

65%* All EU Nationals permanently resident in the UK
60% Non EU Nationals permanently resident in the UK for
a minimum qualifying period of 10 years - subject to management approval on an additional case basis
50% all EU Nationals NOT resident in the UK

* Include 15% M.I.G. Policy above £50,000 Purchase Price
or Property Valuation (whichever is the lowest)

Remortgage Facilities
Remortgages are available for home improvements to the
property, repayment of an existing mortgage on the property
or a transfer of equity. Re-mortgages for any other purpose are
not generally available (i.e. capital raising) and requests would
be subject to Board approval.

Interest Rates

Purchase
A variable margin of 2% - 5% over the variable UK Bank Base
Rate (sterling mortgages)

Remortgage - Available for sterling mortgages only
A variable margin of 3% - 5% over the variable UK Bank Base
Rate.

All advances are subject to status and survey and are calculated on the lower figure of purchase price or valuation.

Further Advances
These are available for home improvement purposes only at
a variable margin of 3% - 5% over UK Bank Base Rate. A
minimum loan of £10,000 applies.

Redemption

Penalty Clause
In the event that the mortgage account is repaid in full within the first two years from the completion date of the initial advance, a penalty of up to three months interest will be levied. The amount of the penalty charge will be added to the total required to redeem the mortgage account.

Mortgage repayment calculation
With effect from April 2000 to April 2001.

Base Rate 5.5%

7.45% per £1.000 (1.95% over the UK base rate)

5 years	£20.25
10	£12.11
15	£ 9.63
20	£ 8.33
25	£ 7.69
Endowment	£ 6.83

5.45% per Euros 1,000 (1.95% over the Repro-European Central Bank)

5 years	19.08 Euros
10	10.83 Euros
15	8.14 Euros
20	6.85 Euros
25	6.11 Euros

A Guide to Fees

Administration Fee

To cover expenses in processing an application, an administration fee is charged of £250. This is payable when you submit your mortgage application. When your mortgage is completed, half of this is refunded to you. However, if you don't proceed with the mortgage, no refund is payable.

Valuation

A valuation from a professionally qualified surveyor will be needed, to check that the property will be good security for your mortgage - and you must pay the fee for this valuation in advance. As soon as the valuation is received, a decision is made. A copy of the report is sent to you.

The valuation fee will be the amount shown in the table below for the purchase price of the property you are buying.

Purchase Price of Property	Valuation Fee
Up to £100.000	£260.
Up to £150.000	£330.
Up to £200.000	£350.
Up to £300.000	£390.
Up to £400.000	£410.
Up to £500.000	£450.
Over £500.000	Quoted individually.

You should note that a valuation is only an inspection of the visible and accessible interior of a property. If you require a more detailed structural survey, tailored to your individual requirements, and upon which you can rely as an indication of the condition of the property, it is recommended that you pay for a more detailed structural report.

Higher Valuation Fees
On the islands of Menorca, Ibiza and Madeira, the survey fees are more expensive, due to the additional travel costs involved. Regardless of the purchase price of the property, the extra fee is usually £120.

Re-inspection Fee
If the surveyor has to revisit the property to re-inspect any details, the additional fee will be £90 (per visit).

Additional Costs
As with buying a property in the UK, *you* will be responsible for paying the legal costs, taxes, and land registry fees. The Abbey National can arrange for local lawyers to give you an estimate of all these costs at the outset - and it is important for you to see this *before* committing yourself to the purchase.

Lawyers' Fees
As the purchaser, you will be responsible for legal fees, as well as your own. In addition, you will be required to pay the relevant taxes, land registry charges and the Notary's fees.

The Abbey National can supply a lawyer from their approved panel if required.

An indication of the legal fees is set out below. In your own interests, you should obtain an estimate from your lawyer, in advance. An indication of the taxes, land registry fees and the Notary's fees can be supplied on request.

For the purchase
1% of the purchase price, subject to a minimum fee of £850 (approximately 212.500 Ptas/€1.277.15 centimos) with an exchange rate of 250 Pesetas to the £, as from 1st March 2002 the exchange rate will be against the Euro and not the Peseta.

Stage payments
If the mortgage is being arranged on a staged payment basis, the scale of fees will be as set out as above, plus :

- If there are to be **two** stage payments: £125 (or 31.250 Ptas/€187.82c., plus IVA and disbursements)

- If there are to be **three** stage payments: £250 (or 62.500 Ptas/€375.64c., plus IVA and disbursements)

Please note, stage payments are not available on apartments.

Subsequent increase in mortgage
Subject to normal lending criteria, you may increase your mortgage at some future date, to help with home improvements or other purposes. The minimum increase is £10,000 - and the legal fees are likely to be :

Amount of loan	Fee
£10,001 to £25,000	£250 or 62.500 Ptas/€375.64c. (plus IVA and disbursements)
£25,000 or more	1% of the amount borrowed (plus IVA and disbursements)

Paying off a mortgage before term
If you pay off your mortgage early, you will incur the following fees :

Legal fees	Administration fee	Other fees
£150 (or 37.500 Ptas/€225.38c.) plus IVA and disbursements)	£200 plus IVA and disbursements	Land registry, Notary, local taxes, plus IVA and disbursements

If you pay off your loan within one year, you must also pay Abbey National Offshore £500 to cover their costs. If you repay your loan during the second year, this fee is reduced to £250. They do not levy any charges for the early repayment of loans which have been running for over two years.

Typical Example

A couple (male and female), both non-smokers, aged 35 next birthday, apply for an Endowment Mortgage of £40,000 towards the purchase of a property priced £63,000. Their regular monthly costs were as follows :

Mortgage interest payment	£316.67
Endowment premium	£88.50
Total Monthly Outlay	£405.17

The cost shown above assumes an interest rate of 9.5% per annum (APR 11.1%) which was a typical rate in June 1998. The rate is variable.

The total costs over the term of the mortgage include the following:

Mortgage interest payment over 20 years	£76,000.80
Valuation	£310.00
Mortgage indemnity fee	£66.00
20 years premiums for buildings insurance (approximate only, index linked)	£2,400.00
Legal fees (for setting up mortgage, approximate only)	£630.00
Final repayment of capital	<u>£40,000.00</u>
Total amount payable over 240 months (excluding endowment premiums)	£119,406.80

Note:

If the property you wish to buy is under construction, the Developer/Builder may well request stage payments. Subject to prudent safeguards, the Abbey National can usually provide a mortgage that matches these requirements, under which two or three stage payments are drawn down as they fall due for payment.

Please note that stage payments are *not* available on apartments.

Life assurance protection and buildings insurance cover will be required. The Abbey National strongly advises people to have a contents insurance also.

Lettings

The Abbey National will have no objection to the property being used for holidays by family or friends - or even occasional holiday lets. However, no long-term or regular letting will be allowed, as this would breach the mortgage agreement.

Mortgages Banca March

The **Banca March** specialises in mortgage facilities in the Balearic Islands, Mallorca, Menorca, Ibiza and Formentera, and the Canary Islands Fuerteventura, Lanzarote, Gran Canaria, Tenerife, Gomera and La Palma.

The **Banca March** has offices at 30 Eastcheap, London, EC3M 1HD (Telephone 020-7 220 7488, & Fax 020-7 929 2446). They will lend in Pounds Sterling or in pesetas and will give a maximum loan of 60% of the valuation. It must be the first mortgage charge on the property, and the maximum term of the loan is between 12-15 years.

Mortgages are repaid on a monthly basis, by direct debit to a current account with **Banca March**, London. The repayment is made in equal monthly repayments of capital, and interest is charged monthly in arrears on reducing capital balance. The interest rate is fixed for the first year at the Libor rate + 1% both for borrowing in Pounds Sterling or Pesetas/Euros. These rates are correct as of June 2001.

You will be charged a set-up fee of 1.5% if the loan value does not change.

The LIBOR rate is reviewed every six months and you will be charged that rate + 1.5% each month until the next review date. You will be charged a set-up fee of 1.5% of the loan value. This is payable when the funds have been made available to you.

Prepayments allowed - 10% of the loan value, with a minimum of £5,000.

Timing of prepayment is permitted at any LIBOR review date, providing you have given at least three months notice.

Other expenses

Professional valuation of the property, to be carried out by *Sociedad de Tasacion* (Society of Professional Valuers) :

Less than 5 million Ptas/€30,050.60c.   12.500 Ptas/€75.13c.

Between 5 million Ptas/€30,050.60c. &
10 million Ptas/€60,101.20c   15.000 Ptas/€90.15c.

Between 10million Ptas/€60,101.20c. &
20 million Ptas/€120.202.40c   20.000 Ptas/€120.20c.

Between 20 million Ptas/€120,202.40c.
& 100 million Ptas/€601,012.00c   20.000 Ptas/€120.20c.

Plus 0.70 per mil on excess over 20 million Ptas/€120.202.40 centimos.

Home Insurance

Buildings: An annual premium of 858 Ptas/€5.15 centimos per million of the official valuation.

Contents: An annual premium of 3.458 Ptas/€20.78 centimos for each million insured.

The approximate costs of the Notary's fees and Land Registry for preparing and registering the mortgage are as follows :

Value of Mortgage	Notary's Fees	Land Registry
5 million Ptas/€30.050.60c.	48.500 Ptas/€291.49c.	19.000 Ptas/€114.19c.
10 million Ptas/€60.101.20c.	54.100 Ptas/€325.15c.	28.000 Ptas/€168.83c.
15 million Ptas/€90.151.80c.	57.900 Ptas/€347.99c.	30.000 Ptas/€180.30c.
20 million Ptas/€120.202.40c.	61.600 Ptas/€370.22c.	42.999 Ptas/€258.43c.

Documentation required :

- Personal information sheet (blank form supplied by the Bank)

- Completed application form (blank form supplied by the Bank)

- Detailed monthly budget (blank form supplied by the Bank)

- A photocopy of your passport

- Your written authority for the Bank to approach your employer for a reference

- Copies of your last three P60's

- Originals of your last three salary slips. (These originals will be returned to you)

- Your written authority to approach your Bank or Building Society for a reference.

- A valuation of the property to be carried out by the *Sociedad de Tasacion*, a firm of independent valuers.

If you are planning to buy a property that already has a mortgage on it, there are two courses of action open to you.

The first option is that you could ask the Bank if the mortgage can be transferred to your name, with you continuing the payments. The second option is that the mortgage can be paid off. If you do not want the mortgage, you must obtain from the Bank in question a written statement of exactly what is owing on the mortgage. You must also ascertain what the cost of the cancellation of the mortgage will be. Once the mortgage has been paid off, the bank in question should ask the Notary's office to prepare a document of cancellation, and a representative of the bank must go along to the Notary's to sign the cancellation of the mortgage. This is then sent by the Notary's office, or the bank representative takes this document to the Land Registry office to remove the mortgage from their records.

The cost of this transaction will vary according to the amount of the mortgage, but can be anything from 100.000 ptas/€601.01c. upwards. So it is most important that you know these costs before you buy a property. Once the amount outstanding on the mortgage and the costs of the cancellation of the mortgage are known, this amount should be deducted from the amount you are paying the Vendor, to ensure that the mortgage is paid and this debt is cancelled at the Land Registry Office. This is probably best dealt with by your lawyer or agent, as the case may be.

CHAPTER 11

Spanish Taxes

Law 40/98 Income Tax of Individuals
Law 41/98 Wealth Tax

Published in the official state bulletin of 5.2.99 and 26.2.99 respectively.

The following tax obligations in Spain are taken from the above mentioned laws. When the regulations governing the law are published, there will be variations in some sections.

The law in force since 1999:

Sale/Purchase of Property

The Vendor : Not residing permanently in Spain

The Vendor is obliged to pay 5% of the declared sale price of the property he is selling and acts as a deposit on account of the capital gains tax, which is charged at the rate of 35% on the difference between the value declared when purchased and the declared value when sold.

The Purchaser is obliged to retain from the Vendor 5% of the declared price of the property purchased and is responsible for making this payment to the local tax office. The Purchaser is totally responsible for this tax (5% of the declared value), this sum being regarded as an encumbrance on the property purchased.

The following are severally responsible for this tax :

The depository or the representative of the property
The taxpayer
The purchaser, for the 5% retained, which must be deposited with the tax authorities within 30 days of the signing of the *Escritura*.

Exemptions

- As from 1 January 1997, property bought by an individual or individuals before 31 December 1986 is free of retention. If the property was bought after this date, i.e. 2 January 1987, the 5% retention applies until the property has been owned for 20 years. However, if the person selling the property is Spanish or is a foreign person with a current *Residencia* card in Spain, and is paying their annual taxes in Spain and can produce a certificate from the Spanish tax authorities proving this fact, the 5% retention does not apply, regardless of the period of ownership. If property was bought by a company on or before 31 December 1976, there is no retention. If a company purchased property after this date, there is a retention of 5%.

- If the transfer of the property takes place in exchange for a life income, provided that the Vendor is over 65 years of age.

- If the transfer of the property is for the following:

  Spanish people or foreign owners with *Residencia* in Spain.

  Death.

Donation to the State, autonomous communities, local authorities, universities, The Spanish Red Cross, The Catholic Church or Public Utility Associations. Also to the Confessional Associations and foundations that fulfil the requirements established by the current legislation.

Where a tax liability is paid by a property that forms part of the Historic Wealth of Spain, according to the current legislation.

Reduction

If the property in question was purchased before 31 December 1994, the capital gains tax will be reduced by 11.11% for each year after the first two years that the property was owned by the vendor, taking into account whether or not improvements have been made. If the property in question was purchased after 31 December 1994, a different discount structure is now applied, according to complicated tables, and to assess any discounts, you would be well advised to consult your *Gestoria* or your Fiscal representative. In fact, to ascertain if you can recover any of the 5% retained, you would need to consult with your *Gestoria* or Fiscal representative.

With regard to reclaiming any, or all of the 5% retained by the purchasers, you must present original copies of your annual tax returns, the Wealth Tax (*Patrimonio*) and Income Tax (which is the tax levied on assumed rental income) and Tax Form 210, (referred to under **Operation** heading overleaf) plus the Tax form 211 which proves that the 5% retained by the purchaser has been paid to the Tax Office. If you have not made these Tax returns each year since you bought your property, or you have not kept the originals, the Tax authorities in Spain will assume that you have not paid these taxes and will deduct them from the amount you are claiming and also levy fines for non-payment, and you could well find that you will get nothing back. You can see that it is very important that you make these Tax returns each year and of course to keep the original copies of them. This is also the case if you have any improvements made to the property, as you may be able to offset this against your capital gain. You must always get official receipts, with the company's official registration number and of course showing that you have paid the IVA (VAT).

Property owned and used only by the owner

Owner : Not residing permanently in Spain

Tax Obligations:

Income Tax

Operation

Ownership of property for owner's own use.
Payment date for tax: From 1 May to 21 June.

Tax Form 210
Tax Base: 2% of the declared value of the property
Tax Rate: 25% of the taxable base, which equals 0.5% of the *Catastral* Value (Rateable Value).
Due on 31 December of each year.

The tax year in Spain runs from 1 January to 31 December each year.

A tax form 210 must be completed for every owner on the *Escritura*.

Wealth Tax (Patrimonio Tax)

Form D-714
Tax base: The value of the tax payer's net property in Spain.

Net property: The difference between the value and the charges which directly affect the estate (property) situated in Spain and which may be exercised against it.

Tax payable: According to scale. This is currently 0.2% of the *Escritura* value. For period ending 31 December of each year.

In total, the tax due on the property is approximately 0.7% of the *Escritura* value each year. The tax is paid in arrears, for example the tax due for the tax year 2001 is paid in 2002.

Fiscal Representative

It would appear that pressure has been brought to bear on the Spanish Government to remove the obligation to have a Registered Fiscal Representative. You are, however, still going to need somebody to deal with your tax returns for you, unless of course you are going to be living in Spain, or are expecting to be in Spain at the time of year when tax returns must be made, which is normally in June.

Drawing on my personal experience, you are well advised to appoint a Spanish *Gestoria* or lawyer to deal with the tax returns on your property. The charges made to act as your Fiscal Representative can vary tremendously, and you really should shop around. I would urge you not necessarily to go for the cheapest quote you are given.

If you do appoint a Fiscal Representative, his/her name must be registered with the local Tax Authorities as your Fiscal Representative.

He/she will then be held responsible for the preparation, presentation and payment of your taxes. The tax year in Spain runs from 1 January until 31 December, so for example, in the year 2002 you will be paying the taxes that pertain to the year 2001 (as previously detailed under **Wealth Tax**.)

Once you have decided on and appointed your Fiscal Representative, he will need your N.I.E. number, together with a copy of your *Escritura* and your signature on a document authorising him to register himself/herself as your Fiscal Representative in Spain. Each person named on the *Escritura* must have an N.I.E. number.

There are quite a number of individuals who act as Fiscal Representatives in Spain, but you are well advised to deal only with Registered Fiscal Representatives, because you are dealing with the Tax Authorities and it makes sense to ensure that your tax returns are completed correctly.

Whatever you decide to do about the returns, the choice is now yours.

Period of time allowed for informing the Tax Authorities

Two months from the date of designation.

Fines

From 25.000 Ptas/€150.25c. to 2.000.000 Ptas/€12,020.24c. for non-observance of your obligations.

Fiscal Identification Number (N.I.E.)

All individuals and companies must have a Fiscal Identification Number for tax purposes. In particular, this Fiscal Identification Number will be required to make the necessary tax returns, and to obtain a Bank Account or Savings Account.

In the case of Foreign owners, this Identification Number is the same as the *Numero Identificacion Extranjero* (N.I.E.) which is issued by the Police.

Notes on the value of the property

The value is understood to be the higher between :

Rateable Value (*Valor Catastral*)
Value of the last transfer
Value the Administration has given the property for any reason.

The Administration makes valuations of properties as follows :

- Supplementary tax demand on the last transfer. The difference between the value the Purchaser declared on the *Escritura* when purchasing and the value according to the tax authorities.

- Payment of tax on inheritance or donations.

- Valuation for other tax purposes, e.g. Municipal *Plus Valia* Tax with reference to land value.

Buildings under construction

The value of buildings under construction is the value of the land, plus all those amounts invested in the construction of the same, including costs and taxes.

Horizontal Property

In the case of *Horizontal Property* - for example: flats, apartments, premises, etc. that form part of a building on various levels, the value is calculated according to the percentage fixed in the title Deed of the property (the quota of participation). The value of the apartment or premises will be according to these conditions.

Multiproperty (Time Sharing)

In the case of partial ownership of a property, the conditions for **Horizontal Property** will apply.

In the case of ownership by any other title, the value will be that of the acquisition of the same.

Rentals: Rental Income

When the owner is either an individual or a corporate body (company)

Rental of Residential Accommodation

The tax is due on the date when the revenue can be exacted, or when the rent is paid, if sooner.

Period for the tax return :

20 working days from the date the tax is due.

Tax Form 210

Tax Base: The amount received for the rental with no deductions of any kind, that is to say the *total rent paid*.

Tax Rate: 25% of the tax base.

Non-resident corporate bodies (companies)

Ownership of Property

Tax Base

The rateable value (*catastral* value) of the property.

Tax rate: 3%

Tax due on 31 December

Payment period: The following month of June.

The following cases will not pay the tax of 3% :

If before 4 August, 1990, the company that is the title holder of the property, residing in a country with an international no double taxation agreement, signed with Spain and if in the said agreement there is a clause of interchange of information.

Companies who can prove the origin of the capital invested and declare who the owners are of the company's capital, and give an undertaking to provide information about any change and its causes to the appropriate authorities.

In my own opinion, this tax law has been introduced to deter people from buying property in Spain in the names of off-shore companies and it makes no sense financially for the average person to buy a property in an off-shore company's name.

Concept of Resident of Spain for Tax Purposes

- When a person stays in Spain for more than 183 days in any calendar year.

- When a person has his principal base in Spain, or the base of his business or professional activities, or of his economic interests.

It will be assumed by the tax authorities, unless proved otherwise, that the tax payer resides in Spain, with his wife, provided there is no legal separation or divorce. It is assumed also that any of his children who are under age and depend on him also live in Spain.

To determine the period of a taxpayer's stay in Spain, his temporary absences are taken into account, unless it is proved that he resides habitually in another country during 183 days of the calendar year.

Companies

- When the company is constituted under Spanish law

- When they have their registered offices in Spain

- When they have their head offices in Spain

Non-Residents with a permanent establishment in Spain

On revenue or capital gains obtained by non-residents through a permanent establishment, a tax of 35% will be levied.

On revenue obtained that is transferred abroad, a further 25% will be levied.

A company is understood to undertake operations in Spain through a permanent establishment, when, either directly or by proxy, it maintains in Spain a management headquarters, branch offices, a factory, workshops, storage installations or assembly plants with a duration of more than 12 months, agencies or representatives authorised to contact in the name of and for the tax paying company, or when it owns mines, quarries, oil or natural gas wells, agricultural, forestry, fishing exploitations, or any other operation for the extraction of natural resources, or when it undertakes professional or artistic activities, or possesses other places of work in which it undertakes all or part of its activities.

Countries with which Spain has double taxation agreements regarding Income Tax

Austria	Luxembourg
Belgium	Morocco
Brazil	Norway
Canada	Poland
Czechoslovakia	Portugal
Denmark	Romania
Finland	Russia
France	Sweden
Germany	Switzerland
Holland	Tunisia

Hungary	United Kingdom
Italy	United States of America
Japan	

This information has been elaborated, studying the laws 18/91 and 19/91 of 1991. Any posterior modification should be taken into account. They are correct as at August 1999.

This information cannot be invoked as a basis for appeals.

The opinions expressed and this information are without prejudice. It is always advisable to check all tax liabilities with a registered Assessor Fiscal, as tax laws are constantly changing in Spain.

N.I.E. Number and Fiscal Representation

As I have stated elsewhere in this guide, you must obtain an N.I.E. number (*Numero Identificacion Extranjero*) and this should be obtained by your estate agent, or lawyer, when they make the application for the *Certificado de No Residente en España*. You need the N.I.E. number for both the Bank and, more importantly, for the annual tax returns that you will have to make.

CHAPTER 12

Selling your Property in Spain

You have decided to sell your property in Spain. Maybe this is because your children have grown up and are off your hands and you don't need such a large property to spend your holidays in; or maybe you are planning to live in Spain permanently and feel you need a larger property. Whatever the reason, this Chapter will explain the procedures.

Most people who have been through the process of selling property in Spain agree that it is not worth all the hassle of trying to sell it yourself - you are much better off giving your property to an estate agent (or agents) to deal with it for you. Generally speaking, estate agents don't expect to get the exclusive rights to the sale of your property and by giving your property to various agents you obviously increase the possibilities of getting it sold. The agent knows the market value of properties in your area and will advise you of the price that you can ask for your property. Another advantage of having various agents valuing your property is that you will be more certain that the value given is a realistic one. You may feel that your property is worth more than the valuation given and of course it is your decision as to the price that your property should be marketed at, but do bear in mind that you could price your property off the market. Be guided by the agents.

As is the norm with selling property anywhere, the agent will take photographs of your property and put them on display in his office window. He will also send out details to any potential buyers and to their overseas agents. Once the estate agent has a buyer for your property and a price has been agreed, a deposit is paid against the signing of a private contract, called a *Compra/Venta* (Sale & Purchase). This commits both parties to the sale & purchase of the property and of course to the price and conditions therein. This means that once the contract is signed, there can be no alteration made to the price, and the date on which the final payment must be made is fixed.

In the contract there are normally two penalty clauses, the first one being that in the case that the purchasers do not complete on the date agreed, they will lose the deposit paid and you, the Vendor, are free to put the property back on the market. The second penalty clause being that, in the case that you, the Vendor, pulls out of the sale after the contracts are signed and the deposit has been paid, you will have to reimburse the purchasers with double the amount paid, as an indemnity. The contract will also reflect the fact that you are responsible for the payment of electricity bills, community fees and so on, up until the signing of the *Escritura* (Deed).

When your property is sold, unless you have a valid *Residencia* (Resident's permit) and you can prove by way of a certificate from the Spanish tax authorities that you are paying your annual taxes in Spain (or you purchased the property on or before 31 December 1986) there will be a retention of 5% of the declared value on the *Escritura*. If your property is registered in the name of a company, there will be a retention of 5% unless the company purchased the property on or before 31 December 1976.

The purchasers must deposit the 5% retained with the Tax authorities in Spain within one month of the signing of the *Escritura*. This 5% retention represents a deposit against your possible capital gains on the property. The capital gains tax is assessed on the difference that you declared you paid on your *Escritura* and the value declared when the property is sold. Certain discounts are allowed against the capital gain, which are determined by the number of years that you have owned the property; the longer you have owned it, the greater the discount becomes. To ascertain what you may be able to reclaim from the 5% retained, you really need to consult with your Fiscal representative in Spain. He/she will advise you on what you can reclaim and will deal with the reclamation. To have an idea of how the discount structure operates, please refer to **Chapter 11 Spanish Taxes**.

You have a period of six months from the date of the signing of the *Escritura* to reclaim against the 5% retained - however it can be anything from six months to a year before you will receive payment.

When the agent has a buyer for your property, under no circumstances allow them possession until the *Escritura* has been signed and full and total payment has been made. If you allow the purchasers possession of your property earlier, there is a danger that they may decide they don't want to buy the property and refuse to leave. You then have the problem of getting them out.

There is also the possibility that your agent has somebody who wants to rent your property for six months or a year, with an option to buy at the end of this period. My advice is to refuse, as it can be fraught with danger. The danger is that they may pay the rent for two months and then stop paying and refuse to leave (and, of course, they probably had no intention of buying the property). Where does this leave *you*? As they have both rental and option to purchase contracts, it is going to take time and cost to get them out of the property. Plus, of course, you are unable to offer your property to anybody else until this situation is resolved. This is the very worst scenario, but it can - and has - happened. If, however, you decide to take the chance and take up an offer of a rental and option to purchase contract, you must get a lawyer to draw up the contracts. As far as the option to purchase is concerned, your lawyer should ask for a substantial sum to be paid for this. The amount paid for the option is deductible from the total selling price if the option is taken up, and forfeited if not. In this way, if the option is not taken up, you at least have some compensation for the length of time that your property has been off the market.

With regard to the final payment for your property, in my opinion the best way to deal with this is to insist that it be made by way of a Bankers Draft, made payable to you. It may well be suggested that the final payment is made by transfer to your Bank on the day of the signing of the *Escritura*. I would say that this is a lot more complicated and it is so much easier for both parties for it to be dealt with by way of a Bankers Draft. Whatever currency you are selling in, the purchasers ask their Bank to issue them a Bankers Draft made payable to you and they bring it with them when they return to sign the *Escritura*.

If, when you put your property up for sale, you feel it may be difficult to get back to Spain for the signing of the *Escritura* to complete on the sale of your property, it makes sense to give Power of Attorney to your lawyer or somebody that you trust in Spain, to deal with it on your behalf. You should organise this *while you are still in Spain*. It really is a simple procedure in Spain to make the Power of Attorney and it is not dramatically expensive, only 7.100 Ptas/€42.67c. (approximately £28.50). You would make what is called a Special Power of Attorney, which authorises your lawyer or your appointed representative to sell your property, sign the *Escritura*, and receive payment. If you decide to make a Power of Attorney when you return to your own country, it is a lot more complicated and certainly more expensive. You will either have to go to the nearest Spanish Consulate to prepare this document, or find a Spanish-speaking Solicitor/Notary to deal with it for you. If it is dealt with by a Spanish-speaking Solicitor/Notary, the Power of Attorney will need an *Apostille* attached to legalise the document in Spain and, of course, it must be in the Spanish language. An *Apostille* is not required if it is signed at the Spanish Consulate in the UK.

Whoever you give the Power of Attorney to, you should insist that the Bankers Draft, for the final payment, is made payable to you and it will be forwarded on to you, unless you want it paid into a Spanish Bank. The estate agent or agents appointed by you to handle the sale of your property will no doubt ask for copies of the following documents :

• A photocopy of your *Escritura* (Deeds)

• A photocopy of the last receipt for the payment of the *Contribuciones*, now known as the I.B.I (Annual Rates)

• A photocopy of the last electricity bill

• A photocopy of the last receipt of the payment of the Community fees (if this applies)

• A photocopy of the last water bill (if this applies)

• A photocopy of the last telephone bill (if this applies)

They may well also request photocopies of your passports & NIE numbers.

They will probably ask you to sign a document authorising them to offer your property for sale with the price agreed.

Lastly, they will need a set of keys for the property, to be able to show prospective buyers. If you are getting keys cut for them, please check first that they work before handing them over to the agent. So often in the past, people have left me keys that were cut especially for my use, and on visiting their property I could not gain access. This was because the keys had been badly cut. So please do check first.

In the past I have found people reluctant to leave me a copy of their *Escritura*. It is very important for the agent to have a copy of your *Escritura*, to enable him to do the necessary searches at the Land Registry office when there is a buyer for your property. It also saves you having to send it to him when he does have a buyer, which saves a lot of time. The copy of your *Escritura* has no value without your signature(s). It will also be necessary for the agent who sells your property to have a copy of your *Escritura* to present at the Notary's to prepare the new *Escritura*.

When your property is sold - that is to say, when a contract has been signed and a deposit has been paid - please do not forget to advise any other agents with whom you placed the property that it has now been sold and arrange to collect the keys from them. You would be amazed at the number of people who sell their properties and forget to advise other agents, and of course they don't collect the keys. As these other agents are unaware that the property has been sold, they continue to show it to people, which can create embarrassing situations: new owners could be in residence, or a client wants to buy and the agent only discovers that the property has already been sold when they contact you. So please remember to advise other agents, and collect the keys, which will be very use-ful for the people buying from you.

CHAPTER 13

General Information

Security

You have bought your property, you are in possession of your *Escritura*, and you are ready to relax and enjoy your new home. Please don't forget to do one more, quite significant thing, because it might be easy, in all the euphoria, to overlook it. This is a reminder to insure your property in Spain - it is very important that you do so.

It is particularly important to insure a property when you own an apartment, because under Spanish Law, you are responsible for any damage to the property below, or a property that *adjoins* your property, if a water leak or something similar occurs.

To give you some idea of the cost of insuring a property in Spanish territory, I asked an Insurance Broker to give me the approximate cost of insuring a property with a value of 15.000.000 Ptas/€90,151.81c. (approximately £60.000) and with contents to the value of 3.000.000 Ptas/€18,030.36c. (approximately £12,000) with the property being empty for up to 3 months of the year and the property being rented out. They quoted me a figure of 52.142 Ptas/€313.38c. per annum, which is approximately £208.

The Insurance Policy covers numerous things, including Acts of God (such as lightening, flooding) as well as robbery. In fact, all the usual things that you would consider insuring against in the UK. The insurance cover you can expect in Spain is very complete. There are plenty of companies offering insurance, including some of the well known names that you will know from the UK, including General Accident, and The Royal. You will certainly have no problems getting insurance for your home in Spain.

If you are not living in Spain permanently, you might want to rent out your property when you're not using it, to recover some of your costs. If you do decide on this, there is no shortage of agencies who would be more than happy to deal with you. Agencies normally take a 15% commission of the rentals, not only dealing with the renting, but also arranging the cleaning of the property and the laundering of bed linen. Obviously, they make a separate charge for cleaning, laundry, gas cylinders and any other costs that they may incur.

The agency should issue you with an annual statement of your account, with rental income and expenses. A good idea would be to ask people you know who already rent out their properties if they can recommend a particular agency. Estate agents can sometimes recommend an agency that they might have connections with. Cowboy agencies, the disreputable ones, are to be avoided at all costs. So, be sure to get a recommendation before you enter into anything.

If you decide not to rent out your property, but would like someone to keep an eye on it while you are not in Spain, look for a reliable agency to give you a management contract. You can expect in the contract :

- A weekly visit
- Airing the property
- Watering plants
- Checking for damp and water leaks

This would cost you in the region of 40.000 Ptas/€240.40c. to 50.000 Ptas/€300.51c. per annum (approx £160 to £200). It is well worth taking out a management contract, as it means the property is being constantly looked over, and should anything like water leaks occur, they are dealt with before any serious damage is done.

Parking in Spain

During the years I have lived in Spain, I have always been aware of, and often exasperated with, the lack of information given concerning parking. The Spanish authorities seem to delight in towing away tourists' cars, subsequently slapping on fines for retrieval. Often the 'culprit' is none the wiser for his misdeed.

Consequently, what follows is an attempt at explanation, to make life a little easier for tourists and non-Spanish speaking residents :

NO PARKING

Red border ring,
red X on a navy blue background

Normally on a metal pole, at the edge of the kerb, or against the wall if it is a pathway

STOP *ONLY* FOR A FEW MINUTES

Red border ring,
single red diagonal line on
a navy blue background

PAY AND DISPLAY PARKING

Square sign on a pole, white background bearing red border ring and a single red diagonal line on a navy blue background. *Look out for the machine issuing tickets*

PROHIBITED TO PARK ON THIS SIDE OF THE ROAD FROM 1-15 OF THE MONTH

Red border ring, single red diagonal line on a navy blue background with 1-15 written in white.

On the opposite side of the road there will be an identical sign bearing 16-31 which, logically, means that you cannot park on *this* side of the road from 16 to 31 of the month.

Other parking restrictions :

You might find a yellow line painted on the edge of the kerb, with a sign similar to the NO PARKING type, bearing one diagonal line and the words **Excepto Carga y Descarga 8h a 13h.** This means that you are not allowed to park during the hours of 8.00 a.m. to 1.00 p.m., because this is an unloading area. You are, however, allowed to park *before* and *after* these times.

Traffic Department / *TRAFICO*

The Traffic Department's procedures are complex and difficult, and you are strongly recommended to use a Consulting Adviser/ *Gestoria*. However, if you prefer, you may do it yourself.

Buying a Car

A foreigner will be able to buy a car in Spain only if he possesses one of the following documents:

* Residence Card

* Property Deeds

* Rental Contract of a dwelling

New Cars

The dealer where you buy the car or an Adviser's Agency/*Gestoria* will take care of effecting the registration, the charge for which is approximately 25.00 Ptas/€150.25c. + Licensing Tax = 13% of the car's value.

Used Cars

Upon buying a used car you will have to:

(1) make a contract of sale; and

(2) effect the transfer of the vehicle

(1)   *Contract of Sale*

This contract can be made by the interested party and it will have to show the following:

- Details of the buyer and of the seller: name, passport/ Residence card and domicile

- Data of the vehicle; model and registration number

- Price of the sale

- Form of payment

- That the vehicle is free of charges

- Date of the contract

- Signatures of the buyer and of the seller

Subsequently, the seller will have to present the original contract and a copy of the contract to *Tráfico* with the copy duly stamped by *Tráfico*, the seller remains exempt of any responsibility for fines, accidents or traffic taxes that the vehicle could have in subsequent years.

You must then present this stamped copy to the Town Hall (*Rentas* Department), so that no future requests for payment of the Vehicle Tax are made to you.

(2)   *Transfer of Previous Title to the New Owner*

To avoid unnecessary journeys and having to make the appropriate transactions in the offices of *Tráfico*, it is preferable that the transfer is undertaken by a *Gestoria*, whose fees are approximately 8.000 Ptas/€48.08c. plus VAT. You may however resolve the matter personally.

The payment of the transfer fee will be made as agreed between buyer and seller. Nevertheless, it is usual for the purchaser to pay.

The amount of the transfer fee will depend on the age and the cylinder capacity of the vehicle. As a guide, a 5 year old Opel Corsa might be approximately 30.000 Ptas/€180.30c. and a 2 year old motorcycle of 250cc some 19.000 Ptas/€114.19c.

Your car has been sold, but you're still receiving demands for vehicle tax . . .

If it is several years since you sold your car and yet you continue to receive the Vehicle Tax demand, this means that the transfer was never carried out. You are still therefore registered as the owner of the car and are responsible for any tax, fine or accident expenses that it could have incurred.

To resolve this situation, it is possible to opt for one of the following solutions:

1.   To pay all the outstanding taxes at the Tax Office/*Oficina de Recaudacion* and de-register the vehicle in the offices of *Tráfico*, presenting the last paid receipt. Subsequently, present a copy of the de-registration to the Town Hall (*Rentas* Department) in order to annul future vehicle receipts.

2.   If your car was not sold, but you no longer possess either the vehicle or the documents, you must take the necessary procedures in the Town Hall (*Rentas* Department) in order to cancel the Road Tax demands. If you are still receiving

demands for road tax, or possibly receiving notice of fines, please contact your *Gestoria* immediately and ask him to get the car cancelled on the *Trafico* computer system - until this is dealt with you are liable for these debts, and interest charges are being added on a daily basis. What is more, bank accounts can be embargoed until such time as payment is made.

BUYING A MOTORBIKE OR MOPED

Purchase of a new motorbike

(A)   *Motorbikes of more than 49 cc:*

This involves the same procedures as for a car.

(B)   *Moped of 49 cc:*

Once you have purchased the motorbike or moped, the registration must be obtained from *Trafico*. This will no doubt be dealt with by the dealer where you bought the motorbike or moped.

Purchase of a second-hand motorbike

(A)   *Motorbikes of more than 49 cc:*

This involves the same procedures as for a car.

(B)   *Mopeds of 49 cc:*

To effect the transfer of the motorbike or moped, this must

be dealt with in the offices of *Trafico*. The best way to deal with this is to contact a *Gestoria*, who will advise you on the documentation required and the cost of the transfer.

Technical Inspection of Vehicles : I.T.V. (MOT)

All cars, vans and motorbikes of more than 49 cc are obliged to undergo an inspection periodically. Also, it is not permitted to buy, to sell or to insure a vehicle that does not have an up to date ITV certificate.

It is necessary to present the Traffic Permit and the Technical Inspection Card.

• A new car will have to undergo the inspection after 4 years

• A car of 4 to 10 years will have to undergo the inspection every 2 years

• A car of more than 10 years will have to undergo the inspection each year

Cars: (Petrol) 4.463 Ptas/€26.82c.
Cars: (Diesel) 5.072 Ptas/€30.48c.

Vans: (Petrol) 4.858 Ptas/€29.20c.
Vans: (Diesel) 5.467 Ptas/€32.86c.

Motorbikes of more than 49 cc:

• A new motorbike will have to undergo the inspection after 5 years

- A motorbike of 4 to 10 years will have to undergo the inspection every 2 years

- A motorbike of more than 10 years will have to undergo the inspection each year

PRICE: 2.145 Ptas/€12.89c.

Vehicles with foreign registration

A car with a foreign registration will not be permitted to stay in Spain more than 6 months in any calendar year. Beyond this time, the car will have to be removed from Spain or change its registration for a Spanish registration.

Also it is possible to request an extension of 6 months, as long as the owner can prove having sufficient economic means for this period.

Changing from foreign registration to Spanish registration

This is a very complex procedure and it is advisable that it is accomplished through a *Gestoria*. The fees for this work will be approximately 50.000 Ptas/€300.51c. plus IVA, besides the charges of *Tráfico* and Customs.

My advice would be to sell your car in England and purchase a car in Spain, rather than go through all the hassle of importing your car into Spain, however fond you are of your vehicle. The other problem that you would have is that you would be driving a right-hand drive car, which brings its own problems when trying to overtake on single carriage roads, amongst all the other things that drivers are likely to encounter.

Vehicle Tax / *IMPUESTO DE VEHICULOS*

Anyone owning a vehicle is subject to this tax. The tariffs are approximately as follows:

CARS	of less than 8hp	2.730 Ptas/€16.41c. per annum
	of 8hp to 12hp	7.371 Ptas/€44.30c. per annum
	of 13hp to 16hp	15.561 Ptas/€93.52c. per annum
	of more than 16hp	19.383 Ptas/€116.49c. per annum

| MOPEDS | | 956 Ptas/€5.74c. per annum |

MOTOR-	of less than 125cc	956 Ptas/€5.74c. per annum
CYCLES	of 125cc to 249cc	1.638 Ptas/€9.84c. per annum
	of 250cc to 499cc	3.276 Ptas/€19.69c. per annum
	of 500cc to 1000cc	6.552 Ptas/€39.38c. per annum
	of more than 1000cc	13.104 Ptas/€78.76c. per annum

Vehicle Entrances / *ENTRADA DE VEHICULOS*

Anyone who owns a garage or an entrance permitting the access of a vehicle to a house or a building is subject to this tax. The tariffs are approximately as follows:

INDIVIDUAL GARAGE:

- Up to 3 metres of frontage 10.000 Ptas/€60.10c. per annum
- Each metre of additional frontage 3.000 Ptas/€18.03c. per annum

COMMUNAL GARAGE: (Each garage up to 3 metres of frontage)

- With 2 places   5.000 Ptas/€30.05c. per annum
- With 3 places   3.350 Ptas/€20.13c. per annum
- With 4 places   2.500 Ptas/€15.03c. per annum
- With 5 places or more   2.000 Ptas/€12.02c. per annum
- Each metre additional frontage, shared proportionally among the garages   3.000 Ptas/€18.03c. per annum

Each vehicle entrance should display the *Vado Permanente* sign (Entrance in Use) so that people do not park in front of it. If a vehicle obstructs the entrance, you can call the tow-away truck (*grúa*) to take the vehicle away. This sign costs 4.500 Ptas/€27.05c. It is payable only once and should be requested at the Rentas Department of the Town Hall.

Building Permits / *LICENCIA DE CONSTRUCCION*

A Building Permit must be requested for any construction work, be it inside or outside the house. To do this, before starting the work, the *Departamento de Urbanismo* (Planning Department of the Town Hall) must be approached, and an application form should be filled in.

This budget should include the price of the materials and the labour costs. The cost of electricity, carpentry and suchlike - even if the work is to be carried out by the owner - must be quoted at a professional rate.

REQUESTING A PERMIT

All works must have a licence before commencing the work. This licence can be requested by :

*   The owner of the house

*   A representative of the owner

*   The builder

The representative and/or the builder should present a notarised Power of Attorney/*Poder Notarial* from the owner, issued in Spain or in his country of origin in Spanish or in a bi-lingual Spanish/own language format. This document costs approximately 7.100 Ptas/€42.67c. (in Spain).

Alterations to existing buildings are considered *OBRA MENOR* (small works). For example:

*   Changing floors

*   Changing tiles

*   Building or removing partitions in the interior of the house

*   Placing or removing doors, windows, gratings

*   Tiling a garden or terrace

*   Adding decorative girders/pergolas to a garden or terrace

*   Raising the walls of the garden

These works do not need plans, and after payment the permit is normally granted the same day on which it is requested.

The extension or construction of a new house is considered *OBRA MAYOR* (LARGE WORKS). For example:

• Building a new house

• Extensions, roofs, garages

• Building an additional floor

• Roofing over a terrace or garden

These works need plans approved by the College of Architects.

The architect's fees to draw up these plans vary around 5 to 10% of the value of the work and **DO NOT** include the cost of the building permit.

Tariffs

The cost of the building licence is calculated in accordance to the work budget as follows:

• Work up to 50.000 Ptas/€300.51c. ....
....0 ptas/€0.

• Work from 50.001Ptas/€300.51 to 107.000 Ptas/€643.08c
....5.000 Ptas/€30.05c.

- Work from 107.000 Ptas/€643.08c. to
  200.000Ptas/€1.202.02c ....5.000 Ptas/€30.05c

- Work more than 200.001 Ptas/€1.202.02c. to
  12.000.000 Ptas/€72.121.45c ......5.3% of the work budget

- Work of more than 12.000.000 Ptas/€72.121.45c ,..............
  ....+ 5.8% of the work budget.

Requirements for carrying out any work

The Building Permit is granted by the Planning Department, *Urbanismo* of the Town Hall only if:

- The house is in a legal urbanisation or legal zone

- The volume of the house permits it according to the regulations

- It is approved by the Town Hall

Once the works are finished, they will be surveyed by a municipal technician. If the technician values the building work carried out to be higher than the amount declared when the licence was applied for, you will have to pay the percentage difference on the value you declared and the value given by the technician.

Occupation of Public Way with construction materials

If during the building work, materials, rubble or other waste spills onto the pavement or road, you will receive, on completion of the works, a notice to pay the Public Way Occupation Tax, which amount is between 15 Ptas/€0.9c. & 60 Ptas/€0.36c. per metre each day, depending on the situation of the building work in the municipality.

NOTE: The figures given for Vehicle Tax-Vehicle Entrances & Building Permits were given to me by the Town Hall in Nerja, Malaga, on the Costa del Sol. They inform me that these figures will vary from one Town Hall to another, so please use them as a guide only.

Planning Breaches

If you do not request a licence, or what was built does not correspond with what was requested, you will have breached Planning and will be subject to a fine.

This fine will vary between 1% and 5% of the budget of the work if the construction is legalizable; and between 10% and 20% if the housing is not legalizable, in which case demolition proceedings will be initiated.

Besides the fine, you will have to pay the construction licence of the completed works, which will be evaluated by the technical personnel of the Town Hall.

Recommended Action

Before starting any building work, you should obtain a written quotation, which itemises all the work to be carried out, and should detail the quality of the materials (the type and cost of the tiles, for walls and floors, doors, windows, etc.) from the builder.

The budget should include the following:

- Identification of the company that is to execute the works

- Identification of the applicant

- Description of the projects with the price of labour and materials

- Total price including taxes

- Limit date for finishing the works

- Date and signature of the builder or professional

- Date and signature of the applicant

- Guarantee

- Form of payment

Normally, the budgets are free. During the works, the constructor is responsible for any damage that he or his workers cause to the house or to other persons or houses.

Payment of Local Taxes

Date of Tax Payment

All receipts are annual. Normally Road Tax can be paid from March to May and IBI (*Contribuciones*) from June to September. The time to pay a receipt may vary from year to year. From the date of issue of the receipt, you will have approximately 3 months to pay.

Place and form of payment of the municipal taxes

There are two ways to make these payments:

(1)   *By Banker's Standing Order*

The bank makes the payment and it is the most effective way since it avoids surcharges and the need to have to find out when a given receipt is due for payment.

You will have to fill in an authorisation in the Tax Collection Office/*Oficina de Recaudacion*, where they will give you two copies, one which you must take to your bank.

You will not be able to request a banker's order if there are any pending payments and it is to be applied for before receipts are made payable.

(2)   *At the Tax Collection Office*

If you do not have the payments made by direct debit, the Tax Collection Office will send you a notice when each receipt is due for payment, indicating the final date for payment.

Unpaid Road Tax or IBI (CONTRIBUCIONES)

The receipts that are not paid within the prescribed dates will have a 20% surcharge, plus interest and costs if legal action is taken. After a given time if payment has not been made, the Tax Collection Office will proceed to embargo bank accounts and thereafter to embargo the property.

Census Register / *EMPADRONAMIENTO*

The census is the official record of the inhabitants of a municipality registered at the Town Hall. The electorate census is established from this record, made up of persons over 18 years, all those with the right to vote. The census is of great importance, since depending on the number of inhabitants of a municipality, such will be the economic contribution of the Central and Regional Administration to cover the following services:

> Municipal Services: Local Police, Refuse, Water, Sewerage, Street Lighting, Roads ...

> State Services: National Police, Doctors, Hospitals, Colleges, Civil Guard, Highways, Courts ...

All persons who normally reside in a municipality have the **OBLIGATION TO REGISTER IN THE CENSUS** of that municipality. If a person resides in several localities in turn, he must be registered in the place where he resides for the greatest length of time.

A person may not be registered in two or more municipalities at the same time. Registration is limited to one municipality only.

If a person wishes to live in another municipality, he will have to request from the Town Hall a document showing his removal from the census and then present this document to the Town Hall of the new municipality where he is going to live.

The Registration on the Census is free and it can be obtained at any time of the year.

Requirements for Registration

All foreigners with residence permits are obliged to be registered, as do all Spanish residents. For this, they will have to present their residence card in the Census *Empadronamiento* Department in the Town Hall.

Photocopies or papers showing that a residence permit has been requested will not be accepted.

In this office a form will be filled in with your domicile and your personal data. If you have been residing in another municipality, you must request a de-registration document from the census of that Town Hall and present this in the Town Hall of the area where you are now living.

Advantages of being registered

Persons that are registered will be able :

(1)   If Spanish, to vote or stand in the local, national and European elections. Foreigners will be able to vote or stand in these elections, as long as this is agreed in the International Treaties.

(2)   To request cohabitation, residence and registration certificates, which they will need for :

•   collecting unemployment and pension payments

•   requesting medical assistance in the Outpatients Department of the Social Security

•   various procedures with the Administration

Also, a foreigner will need a Residence Certificate to buy a car in Spain, and a Registration Certificate to be a member of the Pensioners Home.

Revision of the Census

The census is renewed every 5 years, and the next revision takes place in 2001. For this, several officers from the Town Hall go from house to house taking the relevant information.

If for any reason they do not visit you, you will have to go to the Census Department of the Town Hall and give the necessary information.

If you were registered in the previous census and your information has not been taken when the new census is being checked, you will be excluded.

Those foreigners whose residence cards have expired and who within 6 months have not presented an up to date card to the Census Department at the Town Hall will also be excluded.

Checking that you are registered

In order to check that you are registered, it is necessary to present yourself in the Census *Empadronamiento* Department at the Town Hall to be sure that you are included in the census. This checking is essential at election time since if you are not included in the census, or if there are any mistakes in your identification data, you will not be able to vote.

Also, if there are changes of address, these must be notified to this Department.

Water

Once you have bought a property, the water contract should be transferred to your name.

There is no charge made for transferring the contract to your name - you should present a copy of the *Escritura* (Deeds), a copy of a previous water bill and your bank account details.

If for any reason you need to replace the existing water meter, maybe because the existing water meter is faulty, you should ask the water board to install a new meter. The cost will be approximately 15.650 Ptas/€94.06c. for a meter of 13mm, plus the cost of materials if it is necessary to make any modifications.

Tariffs for the consumption of water

The minimum charge to pay for a standard type meter up to 15 mm is 1.311 Ptas/€7.88c. every 3 months, an amount that will have to be paid whether the property is inhabited or empty.

This tariff corresponds to 30 cubic metres of water. If the consumption is more than this quantity and does not exceed 60 cubic metres, the price of each cubic metre of additional water is 40 Ptas/€0.24c.

Disconnection of water because of non-payment

Each water bill has a payment term of 1 month. Beyond this period, the Water Company will send a notice by registered letter. If the payment is not made within 15 days following the notice, the water supply will be cut off.

The amount to connect the water again is approximately 3.828 Ptas/€23.00c. plus the outstanding debt.

Electricity

Upon buying a house, the electricity meter should be put in the name of the new owner.

The following documentation has to be presented to the Electricity Company.

Resale Property

•   Title deed of the property (*Escritura*)

•   Passport/National Identity, Document/Residence card of the new owner

•   Bank account number to pay the bills by standing order

Please note:

The Electricity Board will need to inspect the mains electric fuse box - particularly on older properties - to see if a trip switch system, and an ICP (a current regulator) has been installed. If the property does not have a trip switch system, you cannot transfer the contract for electricity to your name. You must therefore arrange for a qualified electrician to install one for you, the cost of which can vary between 15 - 25.000Ptas/€90.15c. - €120.20c. You will of course need to give your keys to the Electricity Board to carry out this inspection. There is also a charge of between 5 - 10.000Ptas/€30.05c. - €60.10c. to transfer the electricity contract to your name.

New Property

Apart from the above, you must present:

• A *Boletin* of the installation, issued by the *Delegacion de Industria*.

• First Occupation Licence from the Town Hall. This licence will only be granted if the building satisfies all the town planning and habitation requirements

• Payment of 22.295 Ptas/€133.99c. (for a meter of 4,400 watts) approximately.

Tariff

Upon contracting the electricity supply, you may choose the power capacity to be installed according to your needs, taking into account that each power capacity chosen incurs a different tariff.

All the bills have a standing charge that will have to be paid whether the house is inhabited or empty. Aside from this, they will invoice you for the electricity consumed.

As a rough guide, a contract for 4,400 watts will incur every two months a standing charge of 2.491 Ptas/€14.97c. plus the actual consumption.

Disconnection of electricity because of non-payment

Each electricity bill has a payment term of 15 days. Beyond this period, the local Electricity Company will send you a notice by registered letter.

If the payment is not made within 15 days following the notice, the electricity supply will be cut off.

The amount to connect the electricity is approximately 2.953 Ptas/€17.75c. plus the outstanding debt.

It is advisable to give the details of a second address in case you are away at the time.

Telephone

Applying for a telephone

It is necessary to present in the office of *Telefonica*, the following documents:

- Photocopy of passport/residence permit/National Identity Document

- Title deed (*Escritura*) of the property where you wish to install the telephone. If you do not possess a residence permit or property deeds, you will have to present your N.I.E. (Foreigners Identification Number)

Tariffs

The installation charge will be 27.250 Ptas/€163.77c. + IVA. There is a special charge for persons older than 64 years or with total disability who have reduced economic means. This special tariff goes up to 9.375 Ptas/€56.34c. + *IVA*.

Consumption tariffs

All bills have a standing charge which must be paid whether the property is inhabited or empty. In addition, you will be billed in accordance with consumption.

As a guide, a standard telephone will have a Bi-Monthly standing charge of 3.284 Ptas/€19.74c., plus charges for calls made.

Reduced call charges

Calls within Spain are at a reduced tariff Monday to Friday from 22:00 until 8:00 hours; Saturdays from 14:00 and all day Sundays and holidays.

International telephone calls are at a reduced tariff Monday to Saturday from 10 p.m. until 8 a.m., all day Sunday, and National Holidays.

Disconnection of a telephone line because of non-payment

The telephone is cut off 20 days after non-payment of the invoice.

To connect it again, it will be necessary to pay the outstanding bill plus 2.320Ptas/€13.94c. reconnection charge. Within 48 hours, you should be reconnected.

HOW TO MAKE TELEPHONE CALLS

Calls to provinces

It is necessary to dial the appropriate prefix for each province before the actual phone number.

International calls

Dial as follows:

• 00 (international number)

• Then the number of the country
  (Great Britain = 44; France = 33; Germany = 49;
  Norway = 47; Sweden = 46 ...)

• The prefix of the town/city minus the 0 (zero) on the area code

• The number of the subscriber

Doctors

TARIFFS FOR PRIVATE CONSULTATIONS

• Charges for medical assistance in private consultations varies between 2.000 Ptas/€12.02c. and 4.000 Ptas/€24.04c. approximately

• Medical assistance at home ranges between 4.000Ptas/€24.04c. and 5.000 Ptas/€30.05c. approximately

- A consultation with a basic analysis costs approximately 7.000 Ptas/€42.07c.

Medical invoices should NOT include VAT/*IVA*

Banks

Hours of opening to the public

- Banks / *BANCOS*:   Monday to Friday 8:30 to 14:00
  Saturdays (only in winter) 8:30 to 13:00
- Savings Banks / *CAJAS DE AHORRAS*: Monday to Friday 8:30 to 14:00

Some banks may have different opening hours.

Requirements for opening an account

Anyone can open a bank account in Spain. It is only necessary to present your passport/residence card/identity card.

The opening of an account is free and it can effect deposits and withdrawals from abroad without limit.

If you wish, you can also open an account in foreign currencies.

All bank accounts, except for Non Residents' accounts, are subject to the withholding of 25% of the interest earned for tax.

Schools

As more and more people are making the decision to live and work in Spain - and sometimes these are families with young children - I am constantly being asked about schools.

Around the coastal areas of Spain there are, of course, English-speaking private schools, where the fees probably vary tremendously. My advice therefore is to find out what private school fees are in the area of your choice. However, if your children are still quite young, my advice would be to get your children into a Spanish State school. After the initial struggle with the new language, they will soon pick up Spanish. It really does depend on their age as to which you decide to opt for. The agent or the lawyer you are dealing with will obviously be able to help you with regard to schooling.

Taking your Pets

It is a relatively simple procedure to take your dog, cat or any other domestic pet into Spain, provided of course that you have the right documentation. You must obtain an Export Health Certificate, obtainable from the Ministry of Agriculture, Fisheries & Food, whose address is: Hook Rise South, Tolworth, Surbiton, Surrey KT6 7NF. Their telephone number is: 020-8330 4411.
It makes sense to make application for this certificate well in advance of your travel, in case there are any delays. It is not compulsory for animals to have a rabies vaccination prior to leaving the UK, but it is essential that they have this vaccination in Spain, so it's probably best to arrange this prior to your departure. If you decide to wait until you get to Spain, any vet will be able to deal with it, and the cost is approximately 1.500 Ptas/€9.02c. (£6.00). In Spain, domestic animals can now have a pet passport, with details of the

pet's name, date of birth, and all vaccinations. Micro-chipping will soon be an obligation.

If you wish to take a horse or pony, it is a lot more complicated than the procedure for domestic pets, but you can of course do so. You would need to contact the Equine Section of the Ministry of Agriculture, Fisheries & Food (as shown above) using the extension number of 8190.

National Holidays

1st	January	New Year
6th	January	Epiphany
	March or April	Easter Thursday
	March or April	Easter Friday
1st	May	May Day
15th	August	Feast of Assumption
12th	October	Spanish National Holiday
1st	November	All Saints
6th	December	Day of Constitution
8th	December	Immaculate Conception
25th	December	Christmas Day

If the holiday falls on Sunday, the holiday will be celebrated on the following Monday.

GLOSSARY OF TERMS

Abogados Lawyers/Solicitors

Administrador de Fincas Administrator of Land. Basically an accountant to deal with paying taxes and keeping accounts for the Community of Owners (*Comunidad de Propietarios*).

Agente de Propiedad Inmobiliaria A registered estate agent who has passed examinations in estate agency law

AGM Annual General Meeting

A.P.I. Number Registered no. with the Local College of Estate Agency Lawyers

Apostille Apostile. An internationally recognised seal legalising documents such as Power of Attorney. Issued by the Foreign & Commonwealth Office in London for use in other countries.

Arrendamiento Sitting Tenants

Asociacion Provincial de Instaladores Association of registered electricians & Plumbers.

Boletin de Instalacion Certificate for the installation of Electric & water meters.

Boletin Oficial del Estado A newspaper issued by the state for legal documents

Cargas Charges

Certificado de Fin de Obra A Certificate that the architect must give you or the developer when the building is completely finished, to make the declaration of the new building at the Notary's Office

Certificado de No Residente en España A certificate declaring that you were not registered as a Spanish resident at the time of purchasing a property in Spain

Certificado Negativo 'Negative' Certificate

Compra/Venta Purchase/Sale. Basically the Sales Contract

Comunidad de Propietarios Community of Owners. A group formed by owners of properties, with a President, Treasurer and Secretary to deal with the everyday running of the estate/complex

Contribuciones (Now under the new name of I.B.I. - Impuestos sobre los Bienes Inmuebles) Annual rates, which are paid through the local Recaudacion Office, sometimes incorporated in the local Town Hall

Copia Simple A copy of the original *Escritura*, minus signatures. This document is sufficient to prove ownership and to be able to obtain a bank loan if required

Cortijo A farmhouse. This is the house on a *Finca*

Declaracion de Obra Nueva Declaring a new building, this relates to the Notary and means that you must go to the Notary's Office to make an *Escritura* declaring the fact that you have now built a house/villa on the land that you already own. If it is a new property but already built, this declaration can be done at the same time as the *Escritura* for the land

Delegacion de Industria Delegation of Industry, the authority which issues the certificate for the installation of the electric & water meters.

Departamento de Urbanismo Planning Department of the Town Hall

Embargo A charge registered at the Land Registry Office for any unpaid debts, which can be actioned by a court order to proceed with the auctioning of the property to recover the debt

Empadronamiento Electoral register.

Escritura Deeds for the property

Expediente de Dominio Document of proof of ownership, issued by the courts in the case that there is no *Escritura* for a property

Finca A farm. Often people refer to their Finca, meaning they have a house in the country, with land

Gestoria No UK equivalent, but basically a person dealing with all kinds of bureaucracy, such as applications for *Residencia*/work permits, driving licences, transferring a vehicle to another name, taxes etc.

Grua Tow-away truck

Hipoteca Mortgage

Impuestos sobre transmisiones Patrimoniales 6% transfer tax, for transferring property to your name at the Land Registry Office

INEM Unemployment and Employment Offices

Informe a form detailing the Local Authority's authorisation of what can be built

IVA VAT

Licencia de Aperatura Opening Licence

Licencia de Obra A building licence which must be obtained from the Planning Department at the local Town Hall for all building work

Licencia de Primera Ocupacion Licence of First Occupation. This licence is obtained from the local Town Hall and cannot be obtained without the Town Hall having previously seen the *Certificado de Fin de Obra* (Certificate of the Termination of the Building). Without this licence you will be unable to get an electric meter installed

Licencia Fiscal Tax Licence

Memoria de Calidades Building specification

N.I.E. (*Numero Identificacion Extranjero*) A personal identification number which must be obtained for registration with the tax authorities in Spain (for foreign residents)

Nota Simple A document issued by the Land Registry Office which is a photocopy of the registration details of the property. It shows who the present owner is and if there are any mortgages or other debts registered against the property

Patrimonio Wealth Tax

Plus Valia A local tax that is payable on the sale of the property. It is a percentage of the increase of the value of the land since it was purchased by the vendors

Poder Power of Attorney. This will be required if you are unable to attend the Notary's Office to sign the Public *Escritura*

Public Notaries Government appointed lawyers who have passed the appropriate examinations. They legalise all kinds of documents in Spain, including *Escrituras*, and Powers of Attorney

Residencia Resident. A *Residencia* in Spain means that you have obtained a resident's card, authorising you to live in Spain permanently with the same rights as a Spanish citizen

Segregacion Segregation - for example, of the plot of land that you are buying from the rest of the land on the estate

Testamento Will & Testament

Valor Castastral Rateable value

LAWYERS OPERATING ON THE COASTAL AREAS OF SPAIN

Costa del Sol

Anderson & Asociados Abogados
Centro El Campanario
Oficina 2
Avda España s/n
Urb. Sitio de Calahonda
29647 Mijas Costa   Tel: 00 34 952 932997
Malaga.   Fax: 00 34 952 934902

Luis Herredia
Alonda de Bazan S-1A
29600 Marbella   Tel: 00 34 952 778196
Malaga   Fax: 00 34 952 821710

Juan Bartolome
Avenida Castilla Perez 5
Edificio Horizonte   Tel: 00 34 952 522153
Nerja, Malaga   Fax: 00 34 952 522094

Bartolome Cantarero Martinez
Casa de Campos 1,
2nd Flr, no. 2   Tel: 00 34 952 214620
29001 Malaga   Fax: 00 34 952 210723

Esther Wilkie
Plaza Abogados
Puerto Sotogrande
Edificio C Puerta 2
11310 Sotogrande   Tel: 00 34 956 790280
(Cadiz-Estepona)   Fax: 00 34 956 790279

Carlos Llanos/Francisco Dopico
Plazas Abogados
Edificio Puerta del Mar
Oficina B1
TVA de Carlos Mackintosh S/N
Marbella   Tel: 00 34 952 829393
Malaga   / 828051 / 828288
(Estepona - Malaga)   Fax: 00 34 952 829513

Domingo Cuadra
Calle Calvario 8
Edificio Marbelsun 1-1-10   Tel: 00 34 952 829144
29600 Marbella   Fax: 00 34 952 828130

Santiago de La Cruz Lopez
Martinez - Echevarria y Ferrero Abogados
Avda. Severo Ochoa 28
Edificio Marina Marbella 8 B-C Tel: 00 34 952 76 50 00
Marbella   Fax: 00 34 952 76 44 76

Jose Luis Chillon Martin
Teresa Perez del Valle
Javier Granizo Zafrilla Abogados
Paseo Maritimo 105
Edificio Victoria Towers 1-D
29640 Fuengirola   Tel: 00 34 952 660846
Malaga.   Fax: 00 34 952 661095

Inmaculada Gonzalez Mena
IGM Abogados
C/Real 91 - 1C
29680 Estepona   Tel: 00 34 952 795969
Malaga   Fax:00 34 952 794021
                        e-mail: inmena@ari.es

Gomez Villares Abogados
Santiago Gomez Perez Monoz
C/San Lorenzo 27-5 A.   Tel: 00 34 952 225087
29001 Malaga   00 34 952 223068
                        Fax:00 34 952 220906

C/San Juan Bosco 2-8 A. Tel: 00 34 952 857719 & 2868824
29600 Marbella   Fax:00 34 952 857207

Both of the above are the same bufet of lawyers and the e-mail
address for both is gvabogados@retemail.es

Costa Blanca

Miguel Angel Piano
Piano y Medio Abogados
Marques de Campos 42
Esc. B3
03700 Denia
Alicante   Tel: 00 34 965 784169
(Alicante City - Valencia)   Fax: 00 34 965 784849

Costa Brava

Aurelia Fortuny
De Fortuny Abogados
Calle Aragon No. 235
Pral. 2a ESC. DCHA
08007 Barcelona   Tel: 00 34 93 4872679
Spain   Fax: 00 34 93 4872694

Almeria

Michael John Davies
Parque Comercial 50
Mojacar   Tel: 00 34 950 472775
Almeria   Fax: 00 34 950 472851

Or

C/ Joaquin Rodrigo 16
Aguadulce Roquetas de Mar
04720 Almeria   Tel: 00 34 950 348248
                                  Fax: 00 34 950 348192

Also:

Canary Islands

Santiago Martin Helva
Jose Medio Abogados
Apartado de Correos 105
Los Cristianos
Arona 386400   Tel: 00 34 922 752343
Tenerife   Fax: 00 34 922 752403

Balearic Islands

Alejandro Feliu
Bufete Feliu Abogados
Paseo Mallorca 2
07012 Palma de Mallorca   Tel: 00 34 971 714849
Mallorca   Fax: 00 34 971 72154

Fernando Caballero Visser
Caballero Lafuente Mercadal Abogados Asociados
Calle Norte 12
Mahon   Tel: 00 34 971 352572
Menorca   Fax: 00 34 971 352146

If you would prefer to deal with a Spanish Lawyer who has offices
in the UK, please contact the following:

Fernando Scornik Gerstein
Contact Name: Alberto Perez Cedillo
32 St James's Street   Tel: 020-7 839 1581/930 3593
3rd Floor
London SW1A 1HD   Fax: 020-7 930 3385

J. Polanco Abad & Asociados

Bishopsgate House	Tel: 020-7 377 8088
5-7 Folgate Street	Fax: 020-7 247 3982
London E1 6BX	E mail: demigpol@aol.com

Maria Dolton
El Pinar
Buxted   Tel/Fax: 01825 733536
Uckfield
East Sussex, TN22 4JS

Spanish lawyers based in the UK are extremely useful for making a Power of Attorney should you need one unexpectedly, or if (through lack of time) this was not possible while you were in Spain.

SURVEYORS OPERATING ON THE COASTAL AREAS OF SPAIN

Costa del Sol

Geoffrey Fielding
The Fielding Partnership
La Carolina
Edificio Aries Local 36A
Crta. De Cadiz KM 178.5   Tel: 00 34 952 826754/827754
Marbella, Malaga   Fax: 00 34 952 829754

Mr J Wright
Hadfield House
Mezzanine Floor   Tel: 00 34 952 791242 (Home)
Library Street   Gibraltar 42020
Gibraltar   Fax: Gibraltar 42026

Balearic Islands

Geoff Campion FRICS
Fieldings Partnership
Apartado 65
07400 Alcudia   Tel: 00 34 971 891614
Mallorca   Fax: 00 34 971 891548

Mr Alastair T Kinloch
Calle San Sebastian 2
Entresuelo B
07001 Palma de Mallorca   Tel: 00 34 971 712245
Mallorca   Fax: 00 34 971 712245
                    Home Tel: 00 34 971 730333

Almeria

Mr P Chesler FSVA
Paseo del Mediterraneo 309
Apartado de Correas 641
04638 Mojacar
Almeria
(Valencia - Malaga)   Tel/ Fax: 00 34 950 478834

Also: *Canary Islands*

Mr Mike Woodhouse
38 Parque Albatros
Costa del Silencio
Arona   Tel/ Fax: 00 34 922 730574
Tenerife   Mobile: 00 34 619058387
(Tenerife - Gran Canaria - Lanzarote)

*Please note that apart from the England-based lawyers, the lawyers'
and surveyors' names and addresses reproduced here have been supplied by the Abbey National in Gibraltar. The author has not dealt
with them personally.*

NOTES

* * *

NOTES

* * *